PRAISE FOR

FREEDOM FORMULA FOR PHYSICIANS

"This book is an important primer for physicians at any stage of their career, but strikes me as especially valuable for physicians coming out of training. Mr. Denniston lays out the basics of how to develop (and, perhaps more importantly, implement) a financial plan, and how physicians can rid themselves of debt.

He provides specific tax saving strategies, as well as advanced investment information (building on his earlier work in The Freedom Formula for Young Physicians*). Mr. Denniston concludes by discussing the seven crucial money mistakes every doctor makes, and provides invaluable asset protection advice for physicians.*

I think this book belongs in every physician's library. I would especially recommend it as a 'how to guide' to obtaining financial independence for new physicians"

– DENNIS HURSH

Author of *The Final Hurdle: A Physician's Guide to Negotiating a Fair Employment Agreement*
www.TheFinalHurdle.com

"David has done an excellent job of understanding the unique financial condition of the 21st century physician."

– JENNINGS STALEY, MD
Founder of FreelancePhysician.com

"Doctors' professional lives—packed with clinical duties, education, research, and many other tasks—seldom have time to manage their own lives, never mind the financial aspects of it. With this accessible book, doctors can now address their financial challenges with the same professionalism as they address their patients' needs."

– BETTY TILL

Executive Coach for Physicians and Healthcare Executives

lifeworksolutions.com

"A must read for physicians at all stages of their careers. Freedom Formula for Physicians *eschews tired tips and the same old advice about budgeting to focus on the successful mindset that separates the financially savvy from the paycheck-to-paycheck crowd. Denniston has laser focus on how to make your finances support your life, not the other way around.*"

– RAMSEY TATE, MD

CallMeDr.us

"The Freedom Formula for Physicians *weaves together all the essential elements for building, preserving and growing wealth. Starting with the right mental mindset, then the right investment approach, maximizing tax efficiency and finally how to protect and pass it on to the next generation, David weaves all these together masterfully. Get a copy, read it, practice it and live well!*"

– JOSH METTLE

Author of Why Physician Home Loans Fail

"Unless you have some big fancy economics or MBA degrees behind your name, I believe even those of you physicians or readers who consider yourselves financially literate will benefit from the primer's many insights. Enlivened with personal stories and anecdotes, the book's journey starts by challenging the reader to know where you are, and know where you want to go..."

Instead of pontificating and engaging in political rants, Denniston calmly discusses the implications of updated laws and regulations and how we in the medical community should adapt our financial strategies and tactics. The book offers tools, tables, examples, detailed chapter summaries (for those who like to cut to the chase – although you'd be gnawing on bone instead of enjoying something meatier!) and lists of online and offline resources.

For those of you who can set aside 30 minutes a day to devote to a chapter at a time and work the exercises, and who are committed to gaining control over your financial destiny, this book, especially being tailored to the peculiarities of what we need to own is 'our physician lifestyle', is a worthwhile investment."

– PHILIPPA KENNEALY, MD, MPH ,CPCC, PCC

http://www.entrepreneurialmd.com/

"Physicians are terrific learners by nature and the Freedom Formula helps feed their appetite for knowledge in something we can all (especially Physicians and high earners) learn more about – personal financial health. The book does a great job of the both teaching how to set goals and plan as well as advanced technical analysis and taxes. Dave is clearly an expert in the field and nicely transfers his knowledge to any reader of the book. Freedom does not happen by accident! Highly recommended!"

– JON APPINO

Principal and Founder, Contract Diagnostics
www.contractdiagnostics.com

"He has clearly learned from the reviews I have done of books written by financial advisors in the past—he left out the hard-sell of his services and 'gets' the doctor-specific stuff…"

DR. JAMES DAHLE

Blogger at WhiteCoatInvestor.com

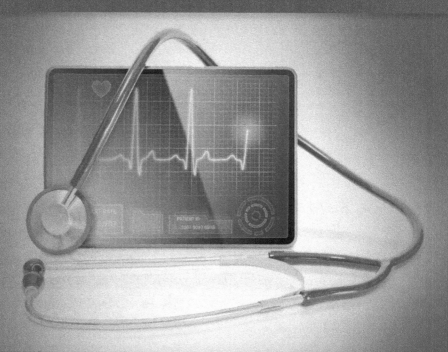

FREEDOM FORMULA
FOR
PHYSICIANS

FREEDOM FORMULA

FOR

PHYSICIANS

A Prescription for
First-Class Financial Health
for Doctors

DAVE DENNISTON, CFA

Published by Advantage, Charleston, South Carolina.
Member of Advantage Media Group.

ADVANTAGE is a registered trademark and the Advantage colophon is a trademark of Advantage Media Group, Inc.

Printed in the United States of America.

ISBN: 978-1-59932-568-2
LCCN: 2015930792

This publication is designed to provide accurate and authoritative information in regard to the subject matter covered. It is sold with the understanding that the publisher is not engaged in rendering legal, accounting, or other professional services. If legal advice or other expert assistance is required, the services of a competent professional person should be sought.

 Advantage Media Group is proud to be a part of the Tree Neutral® program. Tree Neutral offsets the number of trees consumed in the production and printing of this book by taking proactive steps such as planting trees in direct proportion to the number of trees used to print books. To learn more about Tree Neutral, please visit www.treeneutral.com. To learn more about Advantage's commitment to being a responsible steward of the environment, please visit www.advantagefamily.com/green

Advantage Media Group is a publisher of business, self-improvement, and professional development books and online learning. We help entrepreneurs, business leaders, and professionals share their Stories, Passion, and Knowledge to help others Learn & Grow. Do you have a manuscript or book idea that you would like us to consider for publishing? Please visit advantagefamily.com or call 1.866.775.1696.

FOREWORD

by Keith Arbuckle, DPM

Hi there! We haven't met, but I bet we have a lot in common.

I'm Keith Arbuckle, DPM. My field of practice is podiatry.

Before I met Dave, I was lost, trying to navigate the overwhelming sea of information on finances. As did many of my friends and fellow doctors, I accrued a lot of medical school debt.

Along the way, I'd made some big mistakes and I knew I needed help. I needed guidance on my student loans as well as how to invest my money. I came to Dave's seminar and have had the pleasure of getting to know Dave over the past couple of years.

In case you haven't heard of him, Dave Denniston, CFA, is a financial advisor and author who specializes in working with physicians of all ages, whether residents, fellows, physicians who have only recently started to practice, or long-tenured physicians.

Dave loves to help people. His advice has enlightened me and, just as importantly, he's helped me learn from others' mistakes so that I don't have to learn from the school of hard knocks.

His story is pretty crazy. His drive to help doctors came from the birth of his youngest child, Evangeline (Eva). She is his family's little miracle baby. She was born four months prematurely in May 2012 and weighed 12.5 ounces.

She was in the neonatal intensive-care unit (NICU) for nearly five months, which led Dave to embark on a mission to help physicians. The best way to do that was to write, speak, and meet with individuals to offer them financial advice.

He's a bright guy, but more importantly, he's a good guy. He's someone whom I can count on.

I think you'll really enjoy this special book for doctors. Be ready to listen, learn, and grow. He has a lot of information to share with you.

Enjoy!

Sincerely,

Keith Arbuckle, DPM

TABLE OF CONTENTS

INTRODUCTION

"Show me the money!"

"I can't hear you, Jerry . . ."

"Show me the money!"

Tom Cruise shouts these four infamous words at Cuba Gooding Jr.'s character in Jerry Maguire.

As a physician, you've received all kinds of fantastic training in medical school, residency, fellowship, and practice.

Yet, you never received the financial education to understand what to do after you are shown the money. It's a bit like hitting the lotto except, in your case, you earned it through blood, sweat, and tears rather than pure luck.

Along the way, you are getting hit up by salesperson after salesperson who wants to sell you all kinds of financial advice that often involves some kind of insurance product.

Maybe you've received a seminar invitation or two (or three or four or five)?

You are extremely busy, overwhelmed with patients, paperwork from the government, and filling in for your colleagues. You feel you don't have the time or expertise to deal with this financial stuff, but you would like to be at least somewhat knowledgeable.

However, all of that being said, financial planning is absolutely necessary for many reasons, particularly for high-earning doctors who would like to live in comfortable retirement without the pressure of seeing 50 to 100 patients a day.

Maybe you've asked yourself . . .

- I'm tired of all this medical school debt. How can I get on a plan to get rid of all of it?

- I hate paying taxes. They take a bigger and bigger part of my paycheck. How can I give less to Uncle Sam?

- I don't understand investments. What's a philosophy that can help me keep what I have without losing 30 percent of my money every few years?

- How can I protect my family to make sure they don't get screwed by the state or federal government?

If you have ever asked yourself these questions or similar ones, you are in the right place. Explore and learn with me how you can tackle each of these issues and much more.

In this book, I have given you many tools and resources that are practical. Take the next step, which is to read through this book and utilize the resources that are available to you. Use this tool to reflect, strategize, and project yourself into the future.

Are you curious about what other doctors have said about this book and the Freedom Formula? Check out page 217 for more details.

For the most AMAZING gift ever and the COMPLETE Freedom Formula for Physicians System, check out page 220 for more details.

Finally, Dr. Arbuckle mentioned my story and how I came to be so incredibly passionate about helping physicians. You can learn about my miracle child, Evangeline, in the next couple of pages.

If you would like to have additional support and to learn more about how I can serve you, please feel free to contact me anytime at dave@daviddenniston.com or call me at (800) 548-1820.

Let's take this journey together to get you on the path to financial freedom.

Warm Regards,

Dave Denniston

Thank You from the Author

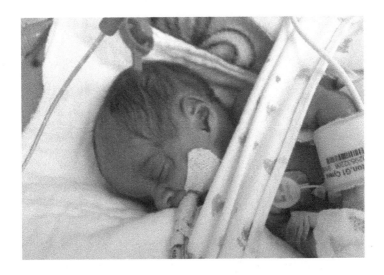

My name is Dave Denniston and I want to thank doctors for the incredible gift of my daughter.

Thanks so much for doing what you do. Let me tell you why I am so grateful to you and your colleagues.

It was May 13, 2012, Mother's Day. My wife, Cyrena, was having an incredibly difficult pregnancy. She had pounding headaches, blurred vision, and searing pain throughout her body.

As a matter of fact, she had been in and out of the hospital for the previous two weeks. Our tiny daughter had gestated only 23 weeks. Her due date was September 9, 2012. Unfortunately, my wife developed toxemia and preeclampsia extremely early in her pregnancy.

Amid tears, she gripped my hand as we were told, "The blood flow is slowing between mom and your daughter. She is fighting, but she is getting weaker and weaker. In our opinion, she needs to come out, but it's your choice."

I asked, "What are the chances of her surviving?" The doctors did not want to tell me. I pressed the question again. With a deep swallow, the doctor in fellowship answered, "Less than 40 percent, but in her case, it is all or nothing. She has several good things going for her."

Here we were, at the crossroads, faced with an incredibly important and mind-numbing decision. This was, literally, a life and death decision. We could get screwed either way.

With a heavy sigh and two heavy hearts, we agreed with the doctor's opinion and asked him to proceed. There I was, trembling, turning around to explain the situation to my six-year-old daughter Gabrielle (we call her Gabby). I got down on one knee. Tears were rolling down my cheeks. I told her, "Gabby, I need you to believe with me. Your sister might not make it today."

Gabby's eyes grew big and started watering. I thought I was going to lose it. Leaving Gabby with a family friend, I went into the surgery preparation room while they got ready for the surgery. Anxiety gnawed at me. I couldn't stop pacing.

Fighting more tears, I was finally brought in the surgery room after what felt like an eternity and was there every step of the way as the wonderful doctors fought to save my wife and my daughter.

An hour and many prayers later, the doctors were right. Our little, tiny baby, barely halfway through the gestation process, made it. She survived!

Born a few ounces short of one pound, she is our miracle baby. We named her Evangeline, meaning "bearer of good news."

This experience forever changed our lives, which, for almost five months from the day of Evangeline's birth, revolved around the hospital where we had the opportunity to get to know many residents and fellows and listen to what they went through.

I began to wonder how I could give back, how I could help the people who saved my daughter's life. I became determined to specialize in working with physicians. My day job is financial counseling. I like to write too, and I have published a few small books.

Since that fateful day in May 2012, I've written small books on a variety of subjects including *Tax Reduction Prescription for Doctors, The Insurance Guide for Doctors, and 5 Steps to Get Out of Debt for Physicians Workbook.*

From time to time, my family and I have continued to visit the NICU clinic. I can't believe how far we have come. I am so grateful to those doctors. I could have lost both my wife and my daughter.

May 13, 2014, was Evangeline's second birthday. She has grown and grown. At this date, Evangeline is no longer suffering the effects of her time in the NICU or her extremely premature birth. She is truly a miracle and the ultimate Mother's Day present.

Let me know how I can help you. My door is always open to doctors. This book is dedicated to my family and the fantastic physicians and other medical staff who saved my daughter's life. My life and my family's life would be different, no doubt for the worse, without you and others like you doing what you do.

Thanks again,

Dave Denniston

CHAPTER 1

PLAN AND PROSPER

The gorgeous blue skies are spotless, un-obscured. The laughter of children peels through the perfect day. People are smiling, chattering, laughing, and playing. There's a lightness to the air.

Yet, one person's mood is darkening the skies, following him like an angry storm about to break. Surely, lightning will come out from that face. A perpetual cloud of a frown covers the face of Dr. Gene Porter.

Gene should be happy. He has a beautiful family and a caring wife. He's been in practice for over 15 years and has amassed a substantial portfolio. He recently changed jobs and moved halfway across the country to Minnesota as a medical doctor of anesthesiology (MDA) for the prestigious Mayo Clinic. The light is at the end of the tunnel and the end of his career is ahead of him!

Yet, he has been covered, he would say buried, under a mountain of debt—$60,000 of undergraduate and medical school debt, plus another $10,000 in credit card debt from spending a bit too much at Christmas. He's been chipping away at the debts slowly but surely, but he can't seem to stay ahead.

On top of that, he just purchased a new car that came with a whopping car loan of $30,000!

He did it all by himself. He pulled up on his bootstraps, taking the money the federal government gladly lent him.

He wonders darkly to himself, "How long am I going to be like this? When will I ever get out of debt?"

So, here Gene is. He is in a tough pickle.

Maybe you are in a similar position, or remember having been in this spot many years ago.

What Gene needs now, more than ever, is a plan and a team to advise him.

What if he had somebody to warn him, somebody to guide him? Perhaps his situation would be substantially different. Maybe he would never have been in this situation if an advisor had given him sound advice and held him accountable.

Unfortunately, as has happened to so many others, he is now in emergency mode. He needs help, and he needs help fast.

This section is dedicated to people like Gene.

Here are the topics we are going to address in this chapter:

- Plan and Prosper
- The Next Step
- Know Where You Are

- Know Where You Want to Go

- The Mastermind

- What Needs to Be in the Financial Plan?

- Monitor, Adjust, and Stay on Track

PLAN AND PROSPER

People turn to financial planners and financial books for many different reasons. The range of personal circumstances is wide.

You opened this book and are reading this page for a specific reason, or maybe for several reasons:

- You are a physician who would like advice on specific strategies for your situation from someone who specializes in working with medical professionals.

- You've realized managing assets and other aspects of your financial life requires knowledge, experience, and time, which you lack, and you're seeking some sort of help.

- Retirement is around the corner and you know you are not financially ready.

- You've just finished your residency or fellowship and have never dealt with a financial advisor. You are looking for input to help get you going.

- You have received, or will receive, significant money from selling your portion of your practice, a property, or you have received an inheritance.

- You are an investment advisor who wants to convey complex financial matters to your physician clients in a way they can understand.

No matter your primary reason for reading this book, I encourage you first to "think and grow rich," as Napoleon Hill so famously put it.

The true secret to financial wealth and success boils down to one thing: your mindset.

You must have the mindset of a financial champion. Your thinking must not be "stankin' thankin'," but must, instead, be fixed on where you want to go. You must constantly make progress in improving your circumstances, day by day, minute by minute.

One of my great passions in my life is track and field. I grew up in Southern California, LA County and Orange County, basking in the glow (and burn) of the constant stream of sunshine. I loved running.

I was never the fastest kid, but I would work my tail off. I made a commitment to be the hardest working person out there so that I could be the best I could be, even though I certainly wasn't blessed with athletic genes.

As a matter of fact, I was the first in my family to ever compete athletically. Regardless, I loved my time in high school in Orange County (Laguna Hills) and collegiate athletics at Seattle Pacific University.

I trained and trained and trained.

My race was the 400 meters. I often joke that one lap around the track is the farthest I would ever run.

The truth is, in my training, I would do that six to 10 times nearly every single day. God, it was exhausting.

Sometimes (okay, always), coming down the final 100 meters, I was panting and heaving and struggling to give it all that I had, to give in that one last kick.

Especially early in the season, I swear I was dragging a piano behind me, struggling the last 25 meters as my body cried out to me, my hamstrings burning; My quads locking up. Yet, I kept on pushing and pushing and never gave up (but it certainly wasn't always pretty).

In my adult life, I've explored this same concept. How can I train myself to earn what I want to earn, to live the life I want to live? How can I continue to be the hardest person working out there and seeing incredible success?

There's no doubt, it ain't easy.

Maybe you're just like me and you find that you have a tendency to be a little critical of yourself, you have a great deal of unused capacity which you have yet to turn to your advantage, but you are always working to become better.

You are disciplined and controlled on the outside, but on the inside you tend to be a bit worrisome and unsure. At times, you've had serious doubts about whether or not you've done the right thing. You pride yourself on being an independent thinker and don't accept other people's opinions without satisfactory proof. You have high aspirations for yourself and set high goals for yourself, only to find other people find them realistic.

I've come to find out I can overcome these mental obstacles by applying this same tactic of training that I applied in track to acquiring wealth. I can mold my mind to acquire wealth. It's so cool that I wanted to share it with you.

Napoleon Hill, in his landmark book, *Think and Grow Rich*, made the outline, the template, for how ANY of us can put our minds to the task.

If you haven't read the book yet, make sure to <u>buy it now!</u>

He asked himself a series of rather simple questions . . . what did the most successful men of his generation (Ford, Carnegie, Rockefeller, Edison) all have in common? What made them financially successful beyond their wildest dreams? What are the ingredients for the "freedom formula?"

First, **Desire.** You must have a burning desire, that inner fire fueling your drive and determination.

Mr. Hill gives an outline where you can simply plug in YOUR desire in the section that covers the principle of **Autosuggestion.** Essentially, you repeat your desires over and over to burn them into your brain, making a regular practice of it and developing a habit.

Another principle, a character trait that Mr. Hill emphasizes, is having **Faith**.

In terms of wealth, that basically means having belief, being able to visualize where you can be in the future even though you aren't there yet.

I definitely suggest checking out his formula. However, I've also developed my own for physicians that you can utilize. Feel free to e-mail me at <u>dave@daviddenniston.com</u> to get a copy of it.

<u>Down below, I give you some very important action steps. Some of this may sound corny, maybe even ridiculous. Writing and repeating things to myself?</u> Do I really have to do all this work?

Yet, here's the deal. Do you want to have the life of an ordinary doctor? <u>Or would you rather have an "extra"-ordinary life set on</u>

target, focusing on having the best possible financial health and living the life you want to live? Take the time to do these exercises and do what others don't do. **I guarantee 90 percent of people won't. I dare you.**

Here are four SPECIFIC steps that I've created especially for physicians to fuel your desires.

1. Close your eyes. Picture yourself 15 years in the future. Are you still in practice? Where are you? Who are you with? What does it look like, feel like, smell like?

2. Think and ponder this question: "What's important about money to you?"

   Think beyond the basics. What drives you? What makes you happy? Why? Then consider this question: "What's important about achieving that state, the way of being?"

3. Identify your biggest goal. It's got to be big! Do you want to retire with $3 million in the bank? Have enough money to start your own practice? Own the building you practice in?

   How does this tie to what's important to you? Make it really specific. Come up with a concrete date. For example, it could be January 1, 2020, or your birthday in ten years by which you will achieve this goal.

4. Design a plan of action for how you can start IMMEDIATELY to work towards this goal. Then, write down your vision and visualize it. Send an e-mail to yourself with the goal. Read your written statement aloud, once per day or twice per day if you can.

See yourself in that place as you read it. Today, you may not fully believe that you can make it there. That's okay; focus on it, commit yourself fully to it, and you'll get there. The power of the repetition is to MOVE your belief, to give you faith. You have to MEAN it, you have to DESIRE it. A burning, insatiable, unquenchable desire. Read it with PASSION, read it with abandonment, read it LOUDLY. Force yourself to believe.

KNOW WHERE YOU ARE

Before you become a client of mine or any other wealth management firm, it is vital to determine the stability of your financial foundation.

A reputable financial advisor will analyze your income, spending, cash flow, tax situation, debt structure, savings, retirement plans, insurance coverage, planned purchases, and asset structure.

This data can be secured through a personal interview, investment statements, debt balances, and tax returns. With this information in hand, your financial professional can assess your financial history. Together, you can estimate future financial changes.

While you may know where you stand financially, most people do not. Simply working through this initial step is often an eye-opening experience. It can reveal why people are not as happy with, or confident about, their finances as they wish to be.

We believe the plan should focus on:

- retirement/transition planning
- cash flow
- diversification

- becoming debt- free

- risk management

- investment strategy

- tax issues

- estate planning

- charitable planning

- where to get help

Here is an example of a couple who once thought their situation was hopeless, but, after creating a plan to address one of the items above, discovered they too could be financially free.

An orthopedic surgeon and her husband from Lake Oswego, Oregon, tried to save money while battling a mountain of debt. They had two young kids, a busy practice, and a mixed martial arts business.

Without a doubt, money was a tremendous strain on their lives.

Because both of them were incredibly successful, each pulling in six figures every year, Uncle Sam took and took and took.

Between payroll taxes, federal income taxes, and state incomes, they shelled out hundreds of thousands of dollars in taxes. They were so frustrated that they could scream. They did not want to pay another dollar to the government. After all, what was the government giving them in return?

Besides the tax issue, there was the mountain of credit card debt, mortgage debt, student debt, and business debt.

CONT.

John, the husband, owned the building where his mixed martial arts studio was. The studio was over $1 million in debt. In addition, it was a variable debt that could change on an annual basis.

The couple worked hard and played hard, constantly trying to improve themselves, but they felt trapped. They were in a rut, not able to get out.

One meeting with me showed them the importance of creating a plan that would light the way to recovery from debt and help them realize their dreams.

Today, four years later, they've doubled their net worth, eliminated their credit card debt, nearly paid off their student debt, reduced the business loan by over $200,000, and are on a plan to save tens of thousands in income taxes.

No matter the situation, it can be changed and improved by creating a financial plan. Do not stop there. Set up a personal advisory team with a trusted financial advisor, a knowledgeable insurance specialist, a sharp accountant, a seasoned attorney, and an experienced business mentor who understands how to succeed in your business. This group is your informal board of directors. They will help ensure that your plan will succeed.

In addition—and this is critical—try to get your advisory team together in the same room, or at least together on a phone call, once a year at minimum so that a healthy dialogue can emerge among these critical people in your life.

The next step is to know where you want to go.

KNOW WHERE YOU WANT TO GO

Once you know where you are now, the next step is to figure out where you want to go. Write the story of your future life as if it had already happened. By adding in all the rich details, you will clarify this vision.

PLAN AND IMPLEMENT

Creating a plan and deciding where you want to go will give you "cause and control" over your future as nothing else will. It will help you keep your perspective in spite of minor setbacks. Creating and following a plan will help bring about happiness and peace because you will be more in control of your destiny.

JOURNAL

Put it all into the story of your future life. I recommend you keep your plan in a notebook or journal that can be purchased in almost any bookstore. Keep the size manageable and the journal handy so you can work on it while you are between meetings, on vacation, or before you go to bed at night.

Start your plan with the end in mind and work backward. First, you create a 10-year vision, then one for three years, and finally, a one-year vision.

10-YEAR VISION

Write the story of your life as you see it in 10 years, as if it has already happened. Add in all the details to make this story or vision real for you. Visualize a typical day in your life exactly 10 years from now.

Which milestones will show you have reached your goal? Ask yourself where you want to be, which roadblocks you must overcome or bad habits you must break, and which nonfinancial goals you want to achieve. Write your answers down to firmly establish them in your mind.

Here are some more questions to ask yourself, but you can make up your own questions as well:

- When do I want to retire?
- When do I want to be debt-free?
- How will I pay for our children's college?
- Do I want to move to a new home?
- What do I want to have, do, or be?
- How can we meet our goals and still enjoy the ride?

The following are nonfinancial key points your vision should address.

WHOM ARE YOU WITH?

Whom do you love and who loves you? What positive people and things do you want to have in your life? What toxic or negative people, influences, and environments need to be eliminated to make the 10-year vision compelling for you?

HOW CAN YOU BETTER SERVE OTHERS?

Serving others is a critical key to being successful and feeling good about it. Ask yourself which groups need your help; what you have to offer; how you can better serve your children, family, or spouse; and whom you can help or mentor.

DO YOUR SPOUSE AND BUSINESS PARTNER(S) "BUY" THE PLAN?

If you are married or have a partner, be sure the vision reflects the desires and goals of both of you. Go to dinner or take a weekend trip with your spouse or partner and create a compelling 10-year vision that excites both of you. Interview each other. Do not stifle the other's vision. Keep the discussion light and in the spirit of possibility. If your spouse/partner truly isn't interested in planning, create the vision alone.

Remember the one who has the clearest vision will control the direction in which the family moves.

Consider doing the same exercise among business partners. If one of you has a second home, visit it, or alternatively, have lunch or dinner with the other partner(s) several times to hash out your common vision. We suggest getting out of the office to do this.

INCLUDE ALL PLANNED PURCHASES AND WHEN YOU PLAN TO MAKE THEM

For example, say you are going to spend $15,000 to remodel your kitchen two years from now, replace your car three years from now, pay for four years of Susie's college education, beginning five years from now, and buy a cabin or second home in nine years. Put these planned expenses in your vision as well.

DOES YOUR PLAN NEED ALTERATIONS?

Your 10-year vision may include staying in your current house until the kids leave or only replacing your cars every six years to build up your savings. It may even involve downsizing to live within your means, get out of debt, and live a more stress-free life. Tell yourself, "I don't want to live by scrimping and pinching pennies." On the same note, ask yourself, "Do I want to be up to my eyeballs in debt with no savings 10 years from now?"

INCREASE YOUR ECONOMIC VALUE

If you plan to make more money, how will you do it? Include what you'll do to improve the economic value of your company. What training can you, your partners, and employees undertake? What skills need to be improved? What certifications should you and others pursue? When are you going to do these things? Who can mentor you?

LEARN FROM PAST SETBACKS

Address all the areas that have sabotaged your plans in the past. If you had a bad business partner, write out the lessons you learned from the experience. If you spent too much and were in financial trouble, write down what you did wrong so you do not repeat past mistakes.

For example, if overspending was caused by remodeling your home, write down what you have learned and what you can do to avoid repeating similar mistakes. If you have friends or associates who successfully handled the same problem, ask them how they overcame it and model their behavior.

After you crystallize your vision of where you are now and create a compelling vision of where you want to be in 10 years, work backward from the 10-year vision to your present situation.

THREE-YEAR VISION

Figure out what you need to do, to be, or to have, in three years, to be on track for your 10-year vision. Be as specific as you can. Remember that the clearer your future vision is, the more likely it is to happen and the more likely you'll be to know if you are off-track.

CURRENT SITUATION VERSUS THE FUTURE

After adding up all future expenses and planned purchases, is there enough money going into savings? Are you realistic about your income increases? Does your past support your view of the future or make it seem unlikely? If you spent more than you made over the last three years, what are you going to do differently so you can save this year? Remember, experience is beneficial and mistakes are inevitable, but learn from these mistakes and do not repeat them.

REDUCE STRESS

If you do not check and recheck your savings and debt management status, money will most likely continue to create stress, not freedom. It is so straightforward to understand, but much more difficult to live. Still, the reduction in stress created from operating true to your plan is priceless. Spending more than you make creates a buildup of debt, a reduction in savings over time, and an increase in stress. In our line of work, we see far too many people depressed about life because they have no control over their spending and debt. We've seen some even turn to drugs or alcohol, effectively masking the pain, and doing nothing to address the underlying problem. Take control here and watch how it entirely changes your overall attitude to life.

LARGEST FIVE BILLS

If spending is a problem, a simple way to reduce the stress is to focus on your five largest bills and come up with specific ways in which you are willing to reduce them. If you are like most people, your largest bills might include your home mortgage, income taxes, cars, business expenses, debt, travel, child support, random purchases, home remodeling/repairs, dining out, and insurance.

Most people, unless focused primarily on reducing their largest bills, cannot afford the little pleasures that make life enjoyable, such as going on a date with their spouse, having a cup of coffee at Starbucks, or belonging to a health club. The results from cutting out the fun stuff usually are the same as going on a starvation diet: you do not lose weight and, over the long run, you just get heavier, or in the case of money, more in debt.

Instead, come up with ideas to reduce at least five major expenses. Then decide on realistic savings ideas you'll truly implement to save at least 10 percent of every income dollar.

As Tony Robbins said in one of his seminars, Date with Destiny (which we highly recommend), "When people do well, they tend to party. When they do poorly, they tend to ponder." Pondering is advantageous, but it is better to set up a personal policy so that you don't repeat past mistakes. Write down exactly what you will change to avoid the same problems. Then, run your solution by someone who has solved that problem in the past.

Write down your three-year plan—where you need to be, what you need to do, and what you hope to have—to ensure that your 10-year vision is real to you and feels achievable.

Does your future require you to spend less? Putting in milestones that do not cost a lot can help keep focus and reduce costs while giving lots of happiness. Some fantastic ideas include learning to play the guitar, going with a church group to help the needy, writing a novel, or taking a bike trip with a good friend.

Do you feel terrific about your 10-year and three-year future? If you do not, go back and rework your 10-year vision until you feel great about it and cannot wait to make it happen.

WITHIN ONE YEAR

Now write the story of your "ideal scenario" one year from now. Describe the milestones required to be on track to achieve this scenario. Depict how you will feel at that point.

- **Write it down.** Does your list of one-year goals look familiar? If it resembles your old New Year's Eve resolutions, what are you willing to do differently to make them happen? Write down what you want, why you want it, and what you are willing to do to make it all happen.

- **Take immediate action.** Do you feel you are drifting away from your spouse? Come up with specific ways you can become closer. Have you addressed ways to improve your health? Come up with steps to eat better and be more active. These may seem unrelated to the topic of money until you consider the costs of divorce and being too ill to enjoy your wealth. Finally, figure out what five things you need to do right now to move toward your one-year ideal.

If there are decisions you have been putting off, decide which path is best for you. This will give you a direction in which to go so you can focus your efforts. Get the balls rolling! Put this entire book on your reading list, do all of the exercises, and commit them to your journal.

- **Review and review.** Break this down even further by reviewing your plan at least quarterly. You are now on a three-month tracking program. It is not just manageable; it is achievable! Write your refinements in your journal every 90 days. Then, once a year, buy a new journal and revise and update your plan. Remember the acid test for wealth accumulation: Are you going in the direction of your goals? Are you on track? Are you saving? Are you paying off debt? If the answer to any of these is no, consider getting help from a professional financial advisor.

THE MASTERMIND

I also strongly suggest you go outside your advisory board or "board of directors" to look for mentorship from your peers.

Whom do you admire? Whom can you learn from?

Napoleon Hill in *Think and Grow Rich* calls this the **Mastermind**.

Basically, you surround yourself with people to keep you accountable, people to help you plan and dream and learn.

I'm part of a mastermind and I get so jazzed every time we interact. I learn something new all the time! Something to make me better, and I have the intention as well to make someone else better.

It's because I'm looking to give as well as receive. It's all about reciprocity.

The mastermind may meet weekly, monthly, quarterly, or once a year. If you really want to grow, meeting more frequently is better than less.

However, something is better than nothing!

In strong masterminds, EVERY person shares a resource and a problem. Always be ready to share, be open, and be honest.

It's not always easy, but you can do it! Take the next step and get involved.

As you get involved in a mastermind, do some leg-work to secure mentors who can help you avoid learning from the school of hard knocks. Find people who are strong where you are weak. Often, it works both ways and you can help them too in some area! In some cases, mentors may even have the power to increase your income and help move your plan.

- **Flock together**. Many doctors find great contacts and conversations come from industry group associations or conferences. I particularly emphasize conferences because they can be a great place to find other doctors and practices that are not regional competitors. This allows a better flow of information because the natural tension of competition is not there.

- **Get it in writing.** Write down what your mentors suggest and ask them to review your plan to see if you missed any key steps. Ask permission to check in with them from time to time to keep on track. You will find most successful people want to help others as long as others maintain responsibility for following their advice and producing results.

- **Recruit experts.** Find mentors who have mastered a particular area in which you need improvement. If they haven't done it themselves, they might lead you in the wrong direction. Interview them. Ask them how they did it. Write down what you learn.

- **Go face-to-face.** During the mastermind, let's say you connect really well with someone who you know can help you—another peer. Give them a call within a week after the meeting and see where it leads. If a phone conversation starts the ball rolling, you should go visit them on site and observe them over a whole day's work. Structure the day around a trip in the area. Look at two or three of their best practices to implement in your practice.

- **Review Plan.** Go over your revised plan with your mentors and advisory team to make sure you heard them properly. Then, do what they suggest. Let them know what worked. Also, let them know what didn't work, as they might know how you can get back on track.

Are you not sure where to start out or where to look to form a mastermind?

Here are some mastermind groups that I would recommend checking out:

1. For physicians in private practice:

   A. GKIC, Peak Performers Group: http://gkic.com/

   B. Celebrity Branding Agency: http://www. celebritybrandingagency.com/

   C. Mike Capuzzi: http://mikecapuzzi.com/

2. For physicians employed by hospitals/ large practices:

    A. Health-care collaboration: <u>http:// healthcarecollaboration.com/mastermind-groups/</u>

    B. Medical Mastermind Community: <u>http:// medical-mastermind-community.com/med/ physician-members-2</u>

WHAT NEEDS TO BE IN THE FINANCIAL PLAN?

To help you increase, keep, and protect your money so you can live from its returns, several key issues need to be addressed.

NET INCOME

What is your net income? Net income is what you get to spend after taxes, payroll deductions, business expenses, and alimony or child support. It is your net paycheck.

You can improve net income by increasing your earned income. Ask yourself, "How can I improve my income by increasing my value to my company, to my employees and partners, or to my customers?" Far too many people simply expect more money without adding any more value. This almost never works, except for an inflationary wage increase or if individuals have just begun their career. More money usually means more work.

Your best defense against a bottom-line cut is to continually strive to do your job better or steer your company into a more lucrative business. Educate yourself or interview someone already getting the financial results you want.

TAXES

It is possible to reduce your taxes or payroll deductions. There are many ways to do this, from reviewing personal expenses that could be used as business expenses, to giving away the "junk" in your attic. In the chapter on tax planning, we'll explore how the tax system works and how to reduce your taxable income before the year is over.

Try to estimate what your net income will be for the next 10 years and outline your plan to increase your net income. If you don't know, guess. You are the only person who has to believe in the plan for it to work. Be conservative with your income guesses and err on the side of underestimating your income.

An easy way to verify what you spend is to take your net income and subtract your past annual savings. Periodically, add up your savings (including your liquid investments) and subtract your debt balances.

If your debt went up and/or savings went down, then your expenses are more than your net income. This is bad. You need to address the poor cash flow.

As an illustration, if Pete, an electrician, increased his debt by $25,000 over the year but his savings stayed the same, he has worsened his financial condition by spending $25,000 more than he makes.

If your savings went up and/or debt went down, you are spending less than that amount.

For example, 35-year-old Anne has $20,000 more in her checking account and $30,000 less debt over the course of a year. That means Anne spent $50,000 less than her net income of $100,000. This is good. Anne is saving 50 percent of her net income.

MONITOR, ADJUST, AND STAY ON TRACK

It is simply not enough to create a great plan. You have to keep it current and updated. The plan must be taken out and reviewed at least quarterly. If you are off track, revise your actions in light of what it takes to achieve your goals.

You're heading in the right direction if you see:

- gross income increasing
- net income increasing
- expenses decreasing
- debt balances decreasing
- annual savings increasing
- portfolio value increasing

You're moving away from your goals if you see:

- debt increasing
- debt payments increasing
- savings decreasing
- expenses increasing
- net income decreasing
- portfolio value decreasing

Don't expect perfection right away. Getting and staying on track is a continually evolving process. When a plane flies from New York to London, it is off-track most of the flight as weather and winds change its course. With each change, the pilot and the plane's computers retarget the plane to its destination until London is ultimately reached. Many of life's roadblocks, such as weather and wind, exist to keep your plan from becoming a reality. The rest of this book addresses key issues and how you can stay on track and reach your destination.

Financial success is that simple. The secret to stress reduction is having a plan and following it.

You can take a simple test and prove it to yourself.

Step 1: Rate your financial stress from one to ten.

Step 2: Create a financial plan and follow it.

Step 3: Retest your financial stress.

You can do this! Take action today and get started.

Get more information! Check out the resources at the end of this chapter.

CHAPTER SUMMARY

You must have the mindset of a financial champion. Your thinking must instead be fixed on where you want to go and to constantly make progress towards making yourself better, day by day, minute by minute.

Napoleon Hill, in his landmark book, **Think and Grow Rich,** made the outline, the template, for how ANY of us can put our minds to the task.

He boiled it down to a couple handfuls of traits.

First, **Desire.** You must have a burning desire, that inner fire fueling your drive and determination.

Mr. Hill gives an outline where you can simply plug in YOUR desire into in the section that covers the principle of **Autosuggestion**.

Next, know where you are. This data can be secured through a personal interview, investment statements, debt balances and tax returns. With this information in hand, your financial professional can assess where you have been in the past and where you will be financially. Together you can come up with best estimates for how these aspects will change in the future.

While you may know where you stand financially, most people do not truly know their position. Simply working through this initial step is often an eye-opening experience that shows why a person is not as happy or secure about their finances as they wish.

Write out your vision for the near future and the far future. Focus on a 10-year, 3-year, and 1-year plan. Track your progress quarterly and adjust your plans annually.

Outside of your advisory board or "board of directors," I also strongly suggest looking to the mentorship from your peers— those you can learn from and those you can teach.

Who do you admire? Who can you learn from?

Napoleon Hill, in *Think and Grow Rich*, calls getting this group of people together the **Mastermind**.

In your financial plan, make sure to focus on your net income and tax situation. Understanding your living expenses and how you can live within your means is the key to unlocking the freedom formula.

An easy way to verify what you spend is to take your net income and subtract your past annual savings. Periodically add up your savings (including your liquid investments) and subtract your debt balances.

RESOURCES

If you would like to enroll in my free video course and receive the report, **Top 5 Financial Tools for Doctors**, make sure to check out my website, www.MDretire.com.

eMoneyadvisor.com (Financial planning software available through me.)

Mint.com (Great for budgeting!)

CreditKarma.com (Learn how to identify pitfalls in your credit.)

Napolean Hill, *Think and Grow Rich*

Masterminds for physicians in private practice:

    A. GKIC, Peak Performers Group: http://gkic.com/

    B. Celebrity Branding Agency: http://www.celebritybrandingagency.com/

    C. Mike Capuzzi: http://mikecapuzzi.com/

Masterminds for physicians employed by hospitals/large practices:

    A. Health-care collaboration: http://healthcarecollaboration.com/mastermind-groups/

    B. Medical Mastermind Community: http://medical-mastermind-community.com/med/physician-members-2

YOU MUST
BE THE CHANGE
YOU
WANT
TO SEE IN
THE WORLD -MAHATMA GANDHI-

WWW.DOCTORFREEDOMPODCAST.COM

CHAPTER 2

FIVE STEPS TO GET OUT OF DEBT

I n order to be debt-free, you must know where you are heading. You know how hard it is to get someplace when you don't have a road map?

I have certainly gotten lost a few times. Thank goodness for GPS in cellphones today!

Let's work together on defining your financial reality and understanding where you want to go on the road map, as well as by when.

You can't plan a trip if you don't know when you are going, as well as where you are going.

In this chapter, we are going to address the following topics:

- Preparing Your Net Worth Statement: "Producing" vs. "Nonproducing" Assets

- Understanding Your Liabilities

- Your Road Map

- Determining Pay-Off Priorities

- Determining Monthly Spending and Where You Can Improve

The exercises in this module are incredibly important in building the cornerstone of your debt reduction plan. For many of us, this can be difficult to look at. Sometimes, we need a guiding hand. Don't hesitate to ask for help if you find you are procrastinating or just can't stand looking at the data on your own.

STEP ONE: PREPARING YOUR NET WORTH

STATEMENT: "PRODUCING" VS. "NONPRODUCING" ASSETS

First, let's understand the difference between producing assets and nonproducing assets.

- **Producing Assets.** Producing assets are investments that are made for the sole purpose of trying to increase your net worth. They usually produce capital gains, dividends, income, or are relatively easy to sell. This includes your accounts at the bank, your investment accounts, insurance contracts, precious metals, and rental real estate.

- **Nonproducing assets.** Meanwhile, nonproducing assets are purchased primarily for pleasure and use. They usually do not produce income and can be very difficult to sell.

This category includes your home (after all, you have to live somewhere!), your second home/cabin, cars, boats, artwork, and hobby collections (e.g., antiques, stamps, etc.).

Next, gather the data you will need for all of your assets. (We'll cover liabilities in step two, but feel free to get those statements as well).

- **Inventory of producing assets.** First, make an inventory of all your producing assets. Get all bank statements (checking/savings/money market/ CDs), investment statements (brokerage account, stocks, bonds, 401(k)s, 457(b)s, 403(b)s, etc.), life and long-term-care insurance policies, and information regarding any rental properties or investment real estate. Use Zillow.com or the last property tax valuation to get an approximation of real estate values.

- **Inventory of nonproducing assets.** Second, make an inventory of all your nonproducing assets, as discussed above.

Utilize the chart on the next page to help yourself get organized. I've included a small sample for your review.

Asset Description	Asset Category	Company	Account Number	Owner-ship	Value	Availability
IRA FBO David	Retirement	Investors Capital	6BB-000000	David	$ 50,000	5/12/2041
Checking	Liquid	Wells Fargo	1234567	Joint	$ 30,000	Now
Savings	Liquid	Wells Fargo	1234568	Joint	$ 5,000	Now
Variable Annuity	Retirement	Transam-erica	123456LBT	Joint	$100,000	1/1/2016
Joint Brokerage	Nonqualified	Investors Capital	6BB-000001	Joint	$ 15,000	Now
Rental Property	Nonqualified	n/a	n/a	Joint	$200,000	Not Liquid

The asset category is divided into three subcategories: liquid, nonqualified, and retirement.

Try to write them down as sorted by the asset category: liquid assets first, then nonqualified, and then retirement. Print out an additional sheet if needed.

- **Liquid assets**. Liquid assets are anything in bank accounts: checking, savings, and money market accounts, and CDs.

- **Nonqualified assets.** Nonqualified assets are assets that you could liquidate without any tremendous tax penalty and don't have restrictions placed on them by the government. They commonly include brokerage accounts, stock awards and options, and real estate investments.

- **Retirement assets.** Retirement assets are assets that give you a tax advantage due to a tax deduction or tax deferral. They commonly include 401(k), 457(b), 403(b), IRA, and Roth IRA accounts, annuities, and cash value life insurance. Make sure to find out if your life insurance policy has a cash value, which usually applies to universal life, whole life, and variable life policies. Term insurance policies do not have a cash value and should not be included as an asset.

Another column on the chart is **availability**. This is the ability to withdraw the funds without worrying about penalties. For example, you cannot withdraw funds from IRAs or 401(k)s until you are 59.5 years old without incurring an early withdrawal penalty of 10 percent. Some annuities levy surrender penalties depending on the term limits. Some levy a penalty for withdrawals made within a four-year period; others specify seven years; and some, even 10 years.

STEP 2: UNDERSTANDING YOUR LIABILITIES

These are the debts and loans that we are looking to eliminate. Before we figure out how to get rid of them, we need to identify the loans and make an inventory of them. I really believe that being organized is more than half the battle. After getting this done, you will be well on your way.

We will need the following information about your liabilities: description, company, principal owned, interest rate, maturity date, minimum payment, current payment, loan type (house, consumer, or business), fixed versus variable, and if variable, when it changes.

To be clearer about what we are looking for, here are a few pointers:

- If you have a credit card that you pay off monthly and that does not have a continual balance, you don't need to include it here.

- We include minimum payment versus current payment because some folks pay more than the minimum and we want to make sure you understand the difference. Perhaps, you could pay less to some liabilities and more to others.

- If you own rental homes, consider business debt rather than house debt. House debt is meant to show the tax-deductible debt on your primary residence. Likewise, we consider 401(k) loans, life insurance loans, and student loans to be consumer debt.

- The reason why we consider student loans to be consumer debt is that they stop becoming tax deductible once the borrower's income reaches a certain level. Currently, that level is $65,000 for single people, or $130,000 for married people.

- Lastly, to understand whether a loan is fixed versus variable, the main question to ask is if the interest rate could change sometime in the future. Home equity lines of credit (HELOCs), adjustable rate mortgages (ARMs), credit cards, and business lines of credit are all common examples of variable loans.

Due to the extremely high level of student debt that most physicians hold, many physicians are eligible for several types of forbearance programs and debt-reduction programs. The difficulty lies in choosing among them.

Truly, physicians have a wonderful opportunity to enroll in debt forgiveness programs. Later on, we'll ask you to think about and explore whether a loan forgiveness program may make sense for you.

Here are a few factors that you may want to consider when looking over the possibilities:

- Does the program cover your field of practice?

- Does the program apply only to a specific loan or does the forgiveness program cover multiple loans?

- Is this an employer or a state funded program?

- Are the benefits taxable or not?

- What is the length of the commitment?

- Does the employer or the state pay down the loan each year or wait until the end of the commitment?

Let's look at a couple of examples of debt forgiveness programs.

First, the most common debt program that physicians look into is the 10-Year Public Loan Forgiveness program.

This is sponsored by the federal government and can cover virtually any field of practice. You don't have to specify a specific loan because it can cover all of your loans (assuming they are Stafford, Perkins, or other federally backed programs). The benefits are currently not taxable, but this could change in the future.

As the title of the program indicates, it is a 10-year program. The federal government will not forgive the balance until the end of the program.

HOW THE 10-YEAR PROGRAM WORKS

While you are employed full-time by a public service organization, you must make 120 on-time, full, monthly payments (employment includes residencies and fellowships).

Think about this for a minute. This is just seven years out of a residency, or maybe only three, four, or five years out of a fellowship.

Note that if you have Federal Family Education Loan(s) (FFEL) and/or Perkins loans, you need to consolidate them into a direct consolidation loan to take advantage of the program.

Qualifying employment is any employment with a federal, state, or local government agency or a nonprofit that has a 501(c)3 status. But the program also covers certain nonprofits that aren't 501(c)3s.

Let me emphasize strongly that if you are employed by a hospital that has a nonprofit 501(c)3 status, you are probably eligible for this program.

Be aware of whether the arm you are working for is a nonprofit or a for-profit. Some nonprofit hospitals can have a for-profit subsidiary, for tax reasons.

Note that your monthly payments are substantially lower while in residency and fellowship. Later, we will go through some examples covering after-residency employment and fellowship.

Think about this for a minute.

If you are in residency for three years, you will only have seven years remaining on payments.

Meanwhile, if you have a fellowship for three years in addition to three years of residency, you only have four years remaining on payments.

The bottom line is to make sure you enroll while you are in residency and fellowship.

If you have FFEL and/or Perkins loans, you need to consolidate them into a direct consolidation loan to take advantage of the program. This process will take one to three months to complete, depending upon your situation.

HOW REPAYMENT WORKS

As you complete the direct consolidation loan, you must pick a repayment program. The four most common programs are the Income-Based Repayment (IBR) plan, Pay-As-You-Earn (PER), plan, Income-Contingent Repayment (ICR) plan, and the 10-Year Standard Repayment plan.

In this book, we focus on IBR and PER, as they require lower payments in residency and fellowship, which can lead to greater debt forgiveness.

Next, you start to make on-time monthly payments for the ensuing 120 months.

Make sure every year, or whenever you change jobs, to complete, with your employer's certification, the Employment Certification form.

Submit the completed form to FedLoan Servicing (PHEAA), and the Public Service Loan Forgiveness (PSLF) servicer, following the instructions on the form.

FedLoan Servicing (Pennsylvania Higher Education Assistance Agency—PHEAA) will review your Employment Certification form, ensure that it is complete, and, based on the information provided by your employer, determine whether your employment qualifies for the PSLF program.

DIFFERENCE BETWEEN INCOME-BASED REPAYMENT AND PAY-AS-YOU-EARN REPAYMENT PLANS

The most common program is the Income-Based Repayment (IBR) plan. The second more recent program is the Pay-As-You-Earn Repayment (PER) plan.

IBR and PER both accomplish the same goal of minimizing your student debt payments while in residency/fellowship and having you pay back your student loans at a higher rate once you are making more dough.

REQUIREMENTS

Note that IBR and PER both require a "partial financial hardship." This means payments of a federal student loan under the 10-year Standard Repayment plan are higher than under IBR or PER.

COMMITMENT

The commitment for IBR is a monthly payment of 15 percent of discretionary income whereas, under PER, the commitment is only 10 percent of discretionary income. Note that discretionary income has a very specific definition: your income minus the poverty level as specified in guidelines published by the government.

ADJUSTMENTS

You will be asked questions about your household income—for example, your spouse's income and their school loans, your kids and so on, as those things affect the poverty guidelines.

How does the government determine your income? It looks at your tax return.

This is an important distinction because the government is looking purely at your adjusted gross income (AGI).

This means that it is taking a snapshot of your income after pretax deductions for 401(k)/403(b) contributions, after pretax deductions for health-savings accounts, and after deductions for any active business losses.

Also, this means that if you ended your residency/fellowship in June and started your first contract in July, you would likely not have to start making higher payments until the following year. For example, if you finished your residency in June 2013, your higher payments would not take effect until past January 2014.

However, the payments do not take into consideration your overall student load debt or your age or whether you have a car loan, mortgage, and so on. The student debt load is particularly interesting as we explore debt forgiveness programs.

Below is a table that I composed by entering information on the calculators at studentaid.ed.gov.

Note that I assumed that this hypothetical borrower is married, has no kids, no spousal school loans, the original loans were $20,000 to $30,000 below the current loan amount, and the loans carry an interest rate of 6.8 percent.

Although this borrower could easily qualify for IBR while in residency, the calculator on the website doesn't allow me to calculate the payment at a $200,000 income level, which is a $150,000 loan amount for IBR.

COMPENSATION	LOAN AMOUNT	IBR	PER
$150,000	$150,000	$1,591/mo	$1,061/mo
$150,000	$250,000	$1,591/mo	$1,061/mo
$200,000	$150,000	*DOES NOT QUALIFY	$1,478/mo
$200,000	$250,000	$2,216/mo	$1,478/mo

However, we could safely assume that the payment should be $2,216/month given the example below, because the monthly payment fluctuates with compensation but not with the loan amount.

Note the tremendous difference between IBR and PER: over $500/month at the $150,000 compensation level and over $700/month at the $200,000 compensation level.

See how the IBR or PER amount does not change as the loan amount goes up? This is because it is primarily dependent on income.

There is one big caveat between the two programs. To qualify for PER, you must not have any current student debt that originated before 2007.

How does all of this tie in with loan forgiveness programs? Let's take a look at an example of two physicians, Dr. Smith and Dr. Jones, who began PSLF at the very start of residency. They each had an equal amount of student debt when they came out of medical school.

Dr. Smith has been in residency for three years, has made 36 payments toward PSLF, and has gone right into practice. He is making $150,000 per year.

Meanwhile, Dr. Jones has also been in residency for three years, has made 36 payments toward PSLF, and has also just entered practice. He is now making $200,000 per year.

Let's examine what would happen if each of them enrolled in IBR or PER at the start of residency.

The table below adds up the monthly payments from the previous example and multiplies them over seven years. There is no increase in salary. I'm keeping it simple and flat. The lifetime payments in the table are the combination of interest and principal over those seven years.

COMPENSATION	LOAN AMOUNT	IBR-LIFETIME	PER-LIFETIME
$150,000	$150,000	$133,644	$89,124
$150,000	$250,000	$133,644	$89,124
$200,000	$150,000	*DOES NOT QUALIFY	$124,152
$200,000	$250,000	$186,144	$124,152

At the end of the seven years—assuming continued nonprofit employment—the remaining portion of their debt would be forgiven.

For example, with $250,000 of loans and $150,000 worth of compensation, after seven years in practice, they will have paid about $90,000 in the PER program compared with about $130,000 in the IBR program, assuming taxable income is $150,000.

After Dr. Smith completes 84 remaining payments, now that he is in practice, he will have approximately $225,000 worth of forgiveness with IBR versus $265,000 of forgiveness with PER.

This is why PER is superior to IBR when the student debt forgiveness programs are tied in with them.

Additionally, the higher the loans, the more beneficial PER enrollment will be.

Let's say that you have $250,000 in student loans. Consider this: At an interest rate of 6.8 percent, you are accruing interest of about $17,000 annually, or $1,416 monthly. With PER, you would have been paying $1,478/month, barely tapping into principal.

Then, over seven years, you will have paid about $124,000 and will have debt forgiveness of almost $250,000 of the principal and, likely, tax-free!

Giving up this gift is the tax equivalent of almost $360,000, or $51,000/year over seven years, assuming a 30 percent tax bracket.

Even with IBR, you would still have debt forgiveness of nearly $200,000, or the approximate tax equivalent of $285,000.

Either scheme is wonderful, but PER is better for debt forgiveness purposes.

Remember, as we mentioned earlier, to qualify for PER, you must have student debt that originated after October 2007. This will likely affect residents and fellows who started in 2012, and even more so over the next few years.

WHAT CAN WE CONCLUDE FROM ALL OF THESE PROGRAMS?

If you are working for a nonprofit entity, PER is probably a better option, unless you do not qualify due to the origination of your student debt. IBR will still be a fine choice.

I would strongly suggest *not* putting extra payments toward your debts if you are enrolled in the 10-Year Public Loan Forgiveness program unless you think you may not be ready to make a 10-year commitment to staying in the nonprofit community.

If you are currently working for a nonprofit and are considering transitioning to a for-profit practice after residency, IBR would be my recommendation. Keep in mind that you can make extra payments beyond the minimum that IBR requires to pay it off sooner, once you are in practice.

EXAMPLE OF A STATE SPONSORED FORGIVENESS PROGRAM

There are also many state-sponsored programs.

The following is an example of a current program in Minnesota, the Minnesota Urban Physician Loan Forgiveness Program.

Who can apply to this program?

Applicants are primary-care medical residents, including those working in family practice, obstetrics and gynecology, pediatrics, internal medicine and psychiatry. You would apply between July 1 and December 1 while completing medical residency training.

REQUIREMENTS

Following completion of the residency, the participant must plan to practice for at least 30 hours per week, for at least 45 weeks per year, for a minimum of three years in an underserved urban community.

THE NITTY GRITTY DETAILS

The state will repay up to $25,000 per year of service, not to exceed $100,000, or the balance of the designated loan, whichever is less.

These payments are exempt from state and federal income taxes. $25,000 is the taxable equivalent of $35,700 (assuming a 30 percent tax bracket).

You must serve at least three years or, otherwise, repay the loan plus interest on what the state paid toward your loan.

Gather together the data that you will need for all of your liabilities.

We'll cover how to prioritize liabilities in step three, but for right now, just get the information.

On page 65, we have included an example for your review. Note how nearly every spot has something in it. Of course, fixed loans don't have anything in the final column since that column is only for variable loans.

I entered "n/a" for the maturity date for the lines of credit since there is no definite maturity date.

One of our goals will be to set a specific maturity date once we have identified the loans that are priorities.

If you are confused by this process or need help getting the information together, feel free to give me a call at (800) 548-1820 or send me an e-mail to dave@daviddenniston.com.

THE OPHTHALMOLOGIST

In 2012, my partner Roger and I met a young ophthalmologist and his lovely wife. They had several young kids and another on the way.

They were buried underneath $200,000 worth of student loans and he was transitioning to practice within only a few months.

They wanted to buy a home and save for their kids' college education. How could they balance all these different desires?

Together, we worked through a number of different scenarios and found that IBR was the best format for them. We even identified which loans to pay off first.

They are now happily settled, enjoying life, and not worrying about their debt, because they have a plan of action.

LIABILITY DESCRIPTION	COMPANY	PRINCIPAL OWED $	INTEREST RATE	MATURITY DATE	MINIMUM PAYMENT	CURRENT PAYMENT	HOUSE, CONSUMER OR BUSINESS	FIXED OR VARIABLE	IF VA, WHEN CHANGED?
HOME MORTGAGE	BANK OF AMERICA	$250,000	4.50%	1/1/2032	$1,400	$1,400	HOUSE	FIXED	
HELOC	BANK OF AMERICA	$10,000	2.50%	N/A	$21	$21	HOUSE	VARIABLE	MONTHLY
STUDENT LOAN	SALLIE MAE	$150,000	6.80%	1/1/2033	$1,000	$1,000	CONSUMER	FIXED	
CAR LOAN	BECU	$10,000	5.00%	1/1/2017	$300	$350	CONSUMER	FIXED	
CREDIT CARD	BANK OF AMERICA	$30,000	11.0%	N/A	$125	$150	BUSINESS	VARIABLE	ANNUALLY

STEP 3: YOUR ROAD MAP

Now that we have made your financial reality visible, we have a blank canvas on which to create a map. We know the names of the cities and the states you are going to travel to. Next, we need to figure out how you are going to get there. What are the roads and freeways you need to take to travel there?

It all starts with one basic question: **what tangible goal do you have that requires money and planning to achieve?**

Dream big! Keep realistic, but allow your mind to wander and think of the possibilities. Paint the picture of what your life would look like as you achieve this goal and afterward.

The answer should be based on three questions: What is your goal? How much money will it take? By when will you achieve it?

Take some time to reflect and think about how you will feel once you have achieved your goal.

Goal: Pay off student loans.
Amount: $150,000

-Currently matures
1/1/2032

-Paying $1,400/mo

Achieve by: 1/1/2025

Describe two or three feelings or thoughts you will have when you achieve this goal.

Amazed! Elated!

It will feel awesome!

Can I retire now?

THE ORTHOPEDIC SURGEON AND THE ER DOCTOR

I find that there are two different kinds of people in the world.

Those who enjoy sharing their feelings and being introspective, and those who don't.

I went through this exercise with one of my clients, an orthopedic surgeon and his wife. We talked for about 30 minutes on what was important to them, getting down to the nitty gritty and what really motivates their life.

We then moved onto the same goal exercise described on previous page. They loved it! They were able to talk out their goals in a way they had never thought of before. It helped them to see reality and the possibilities.

As a matter of fact, they told me it was the best conversation they ever had!

Then, there are those on the opposite side of the table. I had an E.R. doctor once review my workbook 5 Steps to Get Out of Debt for Physicians, and his reaction was less than stellar to doing this kind of exercise.

He said something to the effect of, "This touchy-feely stuff isn't for me!"

However, I would encourage you to give it a go—ESPECIALLY if you are married. Talk to your spouse and go through it together!

STEP 4: DETERMINING PAY-OFF PRIORITIES

By now, you have made a balance sheet for yourself that includes all of your assets and liabilities. Also, you have established the framework for your tangible goals and when you want to achieve them.

Here are a few basic ideas to consider in determining your priorities:

- In general, look to pay off consumer debts with the highest interest rate and lowest balance first.

- Specifically, eliminate consumer debts including credit cards, car loans, and student loans. None of these are tax deductible as mortgages or HELOCs are (assuming an AGI of over $130,000 for married folks).

- If possible, move consumer debts to tax deductible debt such as a mortgage, assuming you feel comfortable with your income on a go-forward basis.

- If there is a 3 percent difference or more in interest rates, go after the largest interest rates.

- If there is a difference of less than 3 percent, and five years or less to maturity, consider paying off the loan with the lowest balance.

- Besides making sure you meet minimum payments, put any "above-and-beyond" payments of additional principal all toward only one loan so you can demolish it quickly.

Let's take action to customize these ideas to your specific situation. The next logical step we need to take is reviewing the data from previous exercises and considering the prioritization of liabilities.

IBR COMPARED WITH PER

Review what I discussed to either defer your loan without starting payments immediately (interest will compound) or forbear the loan through an income-sensitive plan such as IBR or a pay-as-you-earn repayment plan such as PER.

IBR and PER are both great loan forgiveness programs. PER requires you to pay less than IBR on a monthly basis and may be a better fit for your situation.

LOWER YOUR PAYMENT

Sign up for an auto-withdrawal if the lender offers a slight interest-rate deduction.

Are you a year or two from entering full-time practice? As we discussed earlier, consider debt-forgiveness programs that are available through potential employers, federal, or state sources.

STEP 5: DETERMINING MONTHLY SPENDING AND WHERE YOU CAN IMPROVE

The final step in our journey is to discover and strategize how much you can put toward debt without substantially changing your lifestyle.

This can be very time intensive if you want to understand every nut and bolt on a weekly basis.

However, it can also be pretty straightforward if you want to look only on a monthly or bimonthly basis.

Buy or sign up for cash-flow/spending-tracking software programs. Common examples include Mint.com, Quicken, and MVelopes, among countless others.

Some are free and others cost money. Some banks and credit cards offer software as well. Explore one or two of these programs.

Choose one and sign up for it. Link in all of your assets and liabilities through the service you selected. This typically means logging in through the financial sources that you use.

The best programs will automatically categorize your expenses. They may not be entirely correct. Consider reviewing the activity or correcting the categories. Common examples that need categorizing include written checks, mom and pop stores, and small restaurants.

Go to the section in the software that puts your monthly spending all together. For example, in eMoney Advisor, it is in the Trends tab. As you look at the data, find two or three ways in which you can lower your monthly expenses. Perhaps consider shopping for lower-cost medical/auto/home insurance. See if you can refinance your mortgage. Cut out a trip to Starbucks, eat out less often, take lunch to work more often, and so on.

Now that we've talked about expenses, the next logical step is to think about ways to increase your income. If you've increased your income and decreased your expenses, you are well down the path to financial prosperity.

How have you increased your income in the past? How can you increase your income in the future? What training or additional education or certification may allow you to gain a promotion at work or become more desirable to other employers or clients?

THE DEBT-FREE SURGEON

One of my physician clients and his wife have done wonderfully over the years. She was a teacher and he was a surgeon. They put themselves through school and saved up over the years. They even raised two great kids who became doctors themselves. They are successful beyond any measure of most people's standards.

Yet, one thing nags at them. One gaping hole bothers them all the time.

They ask me every time we get together, "Do we have enough money?"

They are afraid of not having enough, afraid of having to go back to work, afraid of being destitute after having been so successful. There are quite a few clients who I honestly worry about. These folks are NOT one of them. It's because they focused on one thing early in their lives—transforming their finances to become debt free.

They purposely focused on getting out of debt. <u>Within 12 years of starting practice, they had all of their medical school debt and home loan paid off!</u>

Consider starting your own small business or moonlighting. Many people today sell trinkets or hobbies through eBay or Amazon.com. What are your talents? What are your passions?

Alternatively, check out Nineline.com or Freelance Physician for moonlighting opportunities for physicians. You can be paid $150/

hour or more. One of my physician friends is now making more money from moonlighting than from his full-time job.

What opportunities could be available to you?

Check out more resources at the end of this chapter.

CHAPTER SUMMARY

Producing assets are investments that are made for the sole purpose of increasing your net worth. They usually produce capital gains, dividends, or income, or are relatively easy to sell. They include your accounts at the bank, your investment accounts, insurance contracts, precious metals, and rental real estate.

Nonproducing assets are purchased primarily for pleasure and use. They usually do not produce income and can be very difficult to sell. This category includes your home (after all, you have to live somewhere!), your second home/cabin, cars, boats, artwork, and hobby collections (e.g., antiques, stamps, etc.).

Make an inventory of all your producing and nonproducing assets. Put the producing assets into three categories: liquid, nonqualified, and qualified.

Second, make an inventory of all your nonproducing assets, as discussed above.

Liabilities are the debts and loans that you are looking to eliminate. Before figuring out how to get rid of these, you need to identify the loans and make an inventory of them. After getting this done, you will be well on your way!

If you own rental homes, consider them to be business debt rather than house debt. House debt is meant to show the tax-deductible debt on your primary residence. Likewise, we consider 401(k) loans, life insurance loans, and student loans to be consumer debt.

Truly, physicians have a wonderful opportunity to enroll in debt forgiveness programs.

There are six specific factors that you may want to consider when looking over the possibilities.

The most common debt program that physicians look into is the 10-Year Public Loan Forgiveness program. Your monthly payments are substantially lower while in residency and fellowship.

If you are in residency for three years and you enrolled immediately, you will only have seven years remaining on payments at your higher income level.

If you have a fellowship for three years in addition to three years of residency, you only have four years remaining on payments at your higher income level.

The most common program is the Income-Based Repayment (IBR) program. The second commonest and more recent program is the Pay-As-You-Earn Repayment (PER) program.

IBR and PER both accomplish the same goal of minimizing your student debt payments while in residency/fellowship and having you pay back your student loans at a higher rate once you are making more dough.

PER is far more favorable for loan forgiveness, but it may not be available to some physicians because of when they started medical school.

In general, look to pay off consumer debts with the highest interest rate and lowest balance first.

Specifically, eliminate consumer debts including credit cards, car loans, and student loans. None of these are tax deductible as are mortgages or HELOCs (assuming an AGI of over $130,000 for married folks).

If possible, move consumer debts to tax-deductible debt such as a mortgage, assuming that you feel comfortable with your income on a go-forward basis.

If there is a difference of 3 percent or more between interest rates, pay off loans with the largest interest rates.

If the difference in rates is less than 3 percent and there are five years or less to maturity, consider paying off the lowest loan balance.

Lastly, sign up for free budget-tracking software to keep track of your expenses and stay on target with your goals.

RESOURCES

If you would like to receive the free DVD, **_Financial Planning 101: The Financial Education You Never Got in Medical School,_** make sure to check out my website at www.PhysicianFinancialSecrets.com.

This website also includes a free video for physicians that outlines a roadmap on how they can balance all their priorities, visions, and dreams.

Also, check out my workbook on the subject, **_5 Steps to Get out of Debt for Physicians Workbook_**, with specific exercises and templates for you to complete. It is for sale on Amazon. com.

CHAPTER 3

THE TAX PRESCRIPTION: SIX WAYS TO REDUCE YOUR TAXES

Young or old, high earner or low earner, what do we all hate? Taxes!

We enjoy the things that taxes provide for us: roads, schools, libraries, retirement income, and security.

Yet, we hate 'em. It's in our blood.

They are the reason why our forefathers dumped tea in the Boston Harbor. We don't like taxes.

Yet, there's a good way and a poor way to go about the process of reducing your taxes.

First of all, I have to confess that I am not a tax preparer, nor am I a CPA. I am an independent financial advisor and wealth manager.

Please remember your tax situation is unique and you should run any of these ideas by your tax professional.

That being said, one of the things that frustrates me the most is how "inactive" tax professionals can be. They are great bean counters, but many of them don't help you figure out ways to better harvest the bean crop so you can keep more beans.

Often, investments and taxes are tied hand-in-hand. Every quarter, I talk with many clients about taxes. I've had the pleasure of working with some great proactive CPAs who have unlocked the vast vaults of their knowledge to me so I can share this content with you.

By utilizing some basic strategies, you can keep more of your "beans."

Over the last few years, one of the joys of my life has been coaching soccer and other sports for my nine-year-old daughter Gabby.

Gabby was blessed with a big, fantastic brain (and a great work ethic) that will carry her a very long way. Unfortunately, Gabby also seems to have inherited her dad's awesomely average athletic ability.

Anyhow, as I'm out there running around after nine-year-old and ten-year-old girls, I find that so much of what they need to learn is the fundamentals of soccer.

For example, how to properly knock the ball with their laces rather than their toes. Also, positioning has become more and more important. Making sure the girls know where to be on the field for given situations and scenarios—where they should be for corner kicks and goal kicks.

Honestly, I'm normally a pretty calm, sedated guy. Yet, when it comes to coaching, I get fired up—really fired up. I'm jumping and shouting, pointing and sharing. One day, I got called out by my assistant coach for being a little over the line. It was needed.

But hey, overall, I love those kids and really want them to succeed. I also put my arms around them and lavish the praise, trying to find something to cheer each of them with from time to time.

What's most frustrating about this age group is how the girls can be in completely different places in their skills, ability, and knowledge.

In relation to taxes, some of you need to work on your fundamentals like my soccer team. We talk a lot in the next few pages about how the tax system works and if that's you, you'll find that section incredibly valuable. Others of you may have more knowledge, but could use a couple of strategies and adjustments.

Ultimately, in this chapter I am sharing all this awesome information to help educate you and your family on ways to proactively reduce your taxes, cuz your bean counter more than likely ain't gunna do it for ya.

My job is all about helping you make smart choices with your money, and I believe this chapter will be a standard to measure others against as you speak to financial advisors and tax preparers.

In this chapter, we are going to address the following topics:

- How the Tax System Works
- Five Ways to Reduce Your Income (without Taking a Pay Cut)
- Managing Capital Gains and Dividends
- Being Charitable
- More Deductions and Write-Offs
- Back-Door Roth IRA

The exercises in this module are incredibly important in determining the right, proactive, tax-planning strategies for you. For many of us, this can be difficult to look at. Sometimes, we need a guiding hand.

Don't hesitate to ask for help if you find you are procrastinating or just can't stand looking at the data on your own.

HOW THE TAX SYSTEM WORKS

First, let's understand how our tax system works.

There are many different kinds of taxes: income taxes, property taxes, sales taxes, business and occupation taxes, and much more.

For the purposes of this chapter, we will be focusing on three kinds of taxes: income taxes, payroll taxes, and capital gains taxes for individuals.

We aren't going to get into corporations, estates, or trusts, because they open up a huge Pandora's box that will take up another two or three volumes of this book.

Income taxes can be imposed by the federal government and your state government.

Some states don't have any income taxes (e.g., Washington and Texas), but most do.

The federal and state income tax systems are tiered and bracketed. This means the more money you make, the higher the tax percentage you pay.

They can differ whether you are married, single, or married and filing your taxes separately.

The great news here is that this is the easiest kind of tax to be proactive with. Most of our discussions will center on income taxes.

Tax credits, deductions, and retirement plan contributions all help to offset income taxes at both the federal and the state levels.

We'll talk more about those later.

We'll take a gander at both the married-filing-jointly and single tax brackets because they are the brackets that apply to most taxpayers.

Check out the federal income tax brackets on the following two pages.

Okay, now that you've seen the tables, hopefully your eyes haven't glazed over!

Let me break down an example to help you understand what may at first seem complicated.

SINGLE

Inc. and Short-term Gains	Base Amount tax	2014 Rates	On Inc. over
0–$9,075	0	10%	
$9,076–$36,900	$907.50	15%	$9,075
$36,901–$89,350	$5,081.26	25%	$36,900
$89,351–$186,350	$18,193.75	28%	$89,350
$186,351–$405,100	$45,353.75	32%	$186,350
$405,101–406,750	$117,541.25	35%	$405,100
$406,751 and over	$118,118.75	39.6%	$406,750

MARRIED FILING JOINTLY			
Inc. and short-term gains	Base amt. tax	2014 rates	On inc. over
0–$18,150	0	10%	
$18,151–$73,800	$1,815	15%	$18,150
$73,801–$148,850	$10,162.50	25%	$73,800
$148,851–$226,850	$28,925	28%	$148,850
$226,851–$405,100	$50,765	32%	$226,850
$405,101457,600	$109,587.50	35%	$405,101
$457,601 and over	$127,962.50	39.6%	$457,600

I am going to look at the married-filing-jointly table.

Ignoring state income taxes, exemptions, deductions, and credits, let's say that you and your spouse are married. Together, you have an income of $17,000.

What is your tax? Looking at the table, the federal government taxes income at a rate of 10 percent up to an income of $18,150. With an income of $17,000, you are in that 10 percent income bracket and you will be taxed at a rate of 10 percent, amounting to $1,700.

Okay, so let's say, instead, that you make $20,000 rather than $17,000.

Up to $18,150 of your income is still only taxed at a rate of 10 percent. The balance of your income is taxed in a higher bracket that covers incomes from over $18,150 to $73,800. In that bracket, the rate is 15 percent.

Again, your tax bracket *does not change* for the first $18,150.

It does change for the additional amount above that figure. With an income of $20,000, you would be taxed $1,815 for the first $18,150 of your income *plus* an additional tax at a rate of 15 percent on the remaining $1,850 of your $20,000 income. This would amount to an additional $277.50, for a grand total of $2,092.50.

Your income is currently in the 15 percent bracket, but your effective tax rate is 10.46 percent.

If, instead, you made $73,800, your income would still be in the 15 percent bracket, but you would pay a total tax of $10,162.50, which reflects a tax rate of 13.8 percent.

Do you see how your effective tax rate can move up as your income increases while you stay in your tax bracket?

Also, you want to be very aware of when you may move from one tax bracket to another.

There is a tremendous jump for married couples filing jointly when they go from an income of $73,800 to an income of $73,801. The tax jumps from *15 to 25 percent*. That's a 10 percent jump! That means your effective taxes will grow exponentially (if you are married) for every dollar above $73,800.

If at all possible, wouldn't you rather stay in the 15 percent bracket? But there is more to consider.

I would be remiss if I didn't briefly discuss tax credits and tax deductions in this section.

Tax credits are the best possible kind of friendly, tax-favorable treatment you can have. Essentially, you are getting a dollar back for every dollar credited. Through tax credits, you may be able to get money back on a tax return that showed you had no income and didn't pay into the tax system. I saw this happen with the homebuyer's act in 2009: A client received money from the federal government even though that client had not paid any taxes (due to tax write-offs in the previous year).

There are also tax deductions and exemptions that offset the income you generate.

The most famous of these is the choice between itemizing your taxes (i.e., using the available deductions) and using the minimum standard deduction.

As of 2014, the standard deduction is $6,200 if you are single, and $12,400 if you are married.

Think about this for a minute. It means that if you are married, at a minimum, the first $12,400 that you make will not be liable for federal income tax because it offsets, dollar for dollar, the first $12,400 of your income.

Essentially, if you are making $18,150, you are only paying federal income tax on $5,750, for a grand total of $575.

There is one provision to be aware of here: the standard deduction starts to phase out at $305,050 if you are married and filing jointly, or $254,200 if you are single. If possible, you want to maintain that deduction.

Instead, think of the tax brackets as shown in the "Filing Jointly Tax Rates" table, adjusted for the standard deduction (for married filing jointly).

DAVE'S ADJUSTED MARRIED-FILING-JOINTLY TAX RATES

Inc. and short-term gains	Base amt. tax	2014 rates	on inc. over
0–$12,400	0	0%	
$12,401–$30,551	0	10%	
$30,552 – $86,200	$1,815	15%	$30,551
$86,201– $161,250	$10,162.50	25%	$86,200
$161,251– $239,250	$28,925	28%	$161,250

We've spent quite a bit of time on income taxes. Let's also take some time to understand capital gains taxes.

Capital gains taxes are the taxes paid on investments after they have been sold (assuming that there is a gain). This can occur in real estate, stocks, bonds, small businesses, and much more.

There are two different types of capital gains taxes: long-term and short-term. Short-term capital gains are incurred when you buy and sell an asset within a year, whereas long-term capital gains occur when you hold an asset longer than a year.

LONG-TERM CAPITAL GAINS–JOINT (SINGLE)	2014 RATES
0–$73,800 (0–$36,900)	0%
$73,801–$457,600 ($36,901–$405,100)	15%
$457,601 and over ($405,101 and over)	20%

Short-term gains are taxed at ordinary income rates, as shown in the table on top of page 85, whereas long-term gains are taxed at special lower rates seen in the table at the bottom of page 85.

Thus, you want as much as possible to utilize long-term capital gains, and you want to hold your appreciated assets for at least one year.

Why does the government care?

FOR THE LONG TERM

The federal government is incentivizing investors to make long-term investments. It wants people to put money into start-up companies and venture capital as well as reduce the volatility of the financial markets.

Let's take a look at the table for capital gains rates on previous page.

This is similar to the income brackets but compressed. Do you see how investors could possibly have zero tax on capital gains if they are in the lower brackets?

That's awesome!

SPECIAL CONSIDERATIONS FOR RESIDENTS AND FELLOWS

Consider the implications of this. If you are a resident or fellow and you have inherited stock that has risen in value way higher than the cost basis, the best time to sell it, from a tax perspective, is while you are a resident or a fellow. You may avoid taxes on the capital gain when you consider the standard deduction gives you a free pass on the first $12,400 of your income.

THE FAMILY MEDICINE PHYSICIAN

One of the greatest joys of my life is connecting with doctors of all walks of life.

I was blown away when I met a female physician with a small practice of 80% + margins and pays relatively little in the way of taxes.

She has no employees. No billing specialist. No nurses. No other doctors!

How the heck does she do this?

She practices "voluntary simplicity". Essentially, she believes, buys in, and practices keeping life simple.

Her office is only about 400 square feet. There's no receptionist.

She doesn't accept Medicare or Medicaid. She has even whittled down the list of insurance companies she works with because of their onerous, invasive, time-sucking poli-cies (one wanted to make sure the restroom was up to a certain code!) and she doesn't want that stress.

She has a practice that is nearly a cash practice! She gets paid quickly and easily and is in complete control of her company.

She also has the ability to control her salary, her tax bracket, and can write-off all kinds of great deductions to REDUCE her payroll taxes. For example, she could take a patient out to lunch or dinner and it reduces BOTH her payroll taxes AND her federal income taxes.

Now, if only I could get her to start a defined benefit plan or an owner only 401(k) (see page 101 for more details there) and have a S-Corp...

Alternatively, if you are making more than $450,000 in income, capital gains taxes will *be far more favorable* than ordinary income. At that level, ordinary income is in the 39.6 percent tax bracket!

A long-term capital gains tax at 20 percent is nearly half of your normal income tax bracket!

Let's take a moment to also understand how the Affordable Care Act (ACA, Obamacare) has affected investment income.

Besides pushing up the tax rate in the top income tax bracket from 35 to 39.6 percent, the ACA added an additional tax on investment income.

A provision in the law adds a 3.8 percent tax on the lesser of net investment income, or any excess of the modified AGI over $250,000 if you are married, or $200,000 if you are single.

This means that if you make over $250,000, your capital gains rate is actually 23.8 percent, *not* 20 percent. While this rate is still lower than your income tax rate, it should make you pause before selling positions with capital gains once you are making more dough.

Again, this is another reason to sell appreciated positions while you are in residency or fellowship.

Keep in mind that, for the most part, capital gains taxes are within your control. You can decide when you want to sell appreciated (or depreciated) positions. You can be proactive and look, in a given tax year, to see how close you may be to bumping against a higher tax bracket, and then decide whether or not to harvest those gains.

You have control!

Finally, let's discuss payroll taxes.

They are the social program taxes that support Social Security, Medicare, and Medicaid.

Without a doubt, payroll taxes are the hardest taxes to avoid. There are no standard deductions or itemized deductions or credits that can offset payroll taxes.

They are pretty much out of your control unless you own a clinic in a small partnership or you are a sole proprietor.

What is completely different about payroll taxes is that they are paid by both the employer and the employee.

Also, they are only exercised on earned income.

This means that if you are not working or are retired, you are not paying payroll taxes.

If you are self-employed, you cannot avoid the responsibility. There too, you pay as both employer and employee. If you are an employee, the employer will withhold all of these taxes and send in a check to the Internal Revenue Service (IRS).

The ACA also comes into play here. Once you are making over a certain dollar amount, you pay an additional Medicare tax. However, most employers don't send this in on your behalf.

Many doctors were caught off guard in 2013 when they found out they had to pay more taxes than normal due to the additional Medicare tax.

Check out the table for more details.

PAYROLL TAXES	2014 RATES
0–$117,000 Social Security	6.2% Employer
0–$117,000 Social Security	6.2% Employee
0–Unlimited Medicare	1.45% Employer
0–Unlimited Medicare	1.45% Employee
$250,000 (joint) and >Medicare (new) *$200,000 (single) and >Medicare(new)*	*0.9% Employee*
Total employee <250k	7.65% subtotal
Total employee and employer <250k (joint), 200k (single)	**15.30% total**
Total employee and employer >250K (joint), 200k (single)	**16.20% total**

Let's understand a few things about this table:

- Social Security taxes are currently capped at $117,000 and will rise with Social Security benefits on an annual basis. I imagine this could be a major discussion point in future budget negotiations between Congress and the president. Imagine how your taxes could go up, if there is no cap on Social Security taxes.

- Medicare taxes have no cap. You pay Medicare taxes no matter how high your earned income is.

- The ACA increased Medicare taxes by almost 1 percent on joint incomes of over $250,000, or single taxpayer incomes of $200,000. Again, your employer is likely not withholding this tax. You may need to adjust your withholding to make up for the difference to avoid owing taxes in future years.

Now let's tie this all together.

Let's look at a couple of scenarios, taking into consideration only the standard deduction and no other exemptions, deductions, or credits. This isn't entirely realistic, but it gives you a very good snapshot of how taxes can work.

THE SCENARIO OF DR. JONES WITH $200,000 OF INCOME

Dr. Jones, a married primary-care physician employed by a hospital, earns $200,000. He has no investments.

First, let's calculate his income tax. Dr. Jones and his wife take a standard deduction of $12,400. This means his federal taxable income is only $187,600.

He is currently in the 28 percent tax bracket, with income between $148,851 and $226,850.

However, his effective federal income tax rate is lower. He pays $28,925 (the tax on the amount below the 28 percent bracket), plus $10,849.72 (the tax on the amount above $148,851), for a total of $39,774.72, or an effective tax of 19.9 percent on his total income of $200,000.

Dr. Jones' hospital also withholds and pays payroll taxes right out of his paycheck.

He will pay 6.2 percent Social Security taxes on the first $117,000, for a total of $7,020. The hospital will also pay that same amount to the government; it doesn't come out of Dr. Jones' pocket.

Then, Dr. Jones will pay a 1.45 percent Medicare tax on *all* of his earned income of $200,000, for a total of $2,900.

Let's add this all up. This is a grand total of $49,694.72 in taxes paid on an income of $200,000, or a total tax rate of 24.8 percent.

Let's see how this compares to Dr. Smith.

THE SCENARIO OF DR. SMITH WITH $500,000 OF INCOME

Dr. Smith, a married orthopedic surgeon, owns her own solo practice where she employs several support staff and earns $500,000 per year. She had a very good year in her investments and realized long-term capital gains of $20,000.

First, let's calculate her income tax. Dr. Smith and her husband do not take a standard deduction because their annual income is well above $305,040.

This means Dr. Smith's federal taxable income is *still* $500,000.

With annual income above $457,600, she is in the 39.6 percent bracket. However, her federal income effective tax rate is lower. She pays $127,962.50 (tax on income in the bracket below the 39.6 percent bracket), plus $16,790.40 (tax on income above $457,600) for a total of $144,752.90, or an effective tax of 28.95 percent on her total annual income of $500,000.

As an employee, Dr. Smith also withholds and pays payroll taxes right out of her paycheck.

She pays Social Security tax at a rate of 6.2 percent on the first $117,000 for a total of $7,020.

She is also an employer, and like the hospital in the previous example, her company must also pay an additional 6.2 percent to the government, but it doesn't show on her paystub and so we are not including it in the total that comes "out of her pocket" directly.

Then, she will pay Medicare taxes at a rate of 1.45 percent on all of her earned income: $500,000, *plus* 0.9 percent on all income over $250,000 (joint) for Obamacare, for a total of $9,500.

Lastly, let's not forget that she had investment income: capital gains of $20,000. Let's assume that her capital gains/other investment income were lower than her modified adjusted gross income (MAGI). Because her income is over $250,000 and she is in the 39.6 percent tax bracket, she will owe 20 percent of her capital gains, plus 3.8 percent due to the ACA, for a total of 23.8 percent on the $20,000 capital gains, or $4,760.

Let's add this all up. This is a grand total of taxes of $166,033 on an income of $520,000 (including capital gains), or a total tax rate of 31.9 percent. Now that you understand the basics, I have some tips to help you gain more insight into your specific situation.

TIPS TO GAIN INSIGHT INTO YOUR TAX SITUATION

Get the last copy of your pay stub. What is your year-to-date compensation? What is your annualized compensation?

Hint: Take your current compensation and multiple it by 12, divided by the number of months already compensated. For example, using an end-of-the-month May check, multiply the amount by 12/5.

Get the last copy of your tax return. Gather information from the first two pages of Form 1040, Schedule A, and Schedule D. This data will be very important later!

Review the data. How do your wages compare to your AGI? How does your AGI compare to your taxable income? Are you itemizing or taking the standard deduction? How much do you have in exemptions? Note that Social Security taxes are not usually included here.

What have you learned about your tax situation?

Next, focus on two lines of the second page of the form 1040 of your tax return- line 61 (total tax) and line 72 (total payments). Line 61 will tell you what you owed the government. Line 72 will tell you what you had paid the government

Were you paying enough to the government or were you paying too much? Going to one extreme or the other could have unfortunate consequences.

I feel that a refund of $1,000 to $2,000 is reasonable. This gives you some cushion. How much of a refund are you getting, or how big a payment are you making?

If you get a large refund ($5,000 and above), you are withholding too much. You are essentially lending money to Uncle Sam for free. I am all for being patriotic, but I won't lend much money to our irresponsible government. I know it feels good to get a big "paycheck" when you get your refund. But instead, couldn't you increase your monthly cash flow?

Then you could pay down your debts more quickly, or, perhaps, invest more on a monthly basis.

In order to correct this problem, increase the number of exemptions on your pay stub at work.

Conversely, if you are writing out big checks to Uncle Sam every April, consider decreasing the number of exemptions so that more taxes are withheld. Writing big checks is painful for many of us!

FIVE WAYS TO REDUCE YOUR INCOME (WITHOUT TAKING A PAY CUT)

Now that we've covered the basics of taxes and how they work, let's explore several easy ways to reduce income taxes.

1. Paycheck: Contribute to a 401(k) or 403(b)

I have one basic rule, a mere three words, that I have spoken about in seminars at the Mayo Clinic and with the Minnesota Medical Association time and time again. Pay close attention.

Pay yourself first.

Let's emphasize this again. Everybody now repeat after me . . .

Pay yourself first.

This mantra is simple, yet, for many of us, it can be very hard to apply.

First, just simply get started. Contribute to your 401(k) (or 403(b) for nonprofits, e.g., hospitals). It not only counts toward retirement but it lowers your income taxes.

This money comes right out of your paycheck, withheld by your employer; it never even sees your tax return. This is because the income reported on your tax return is *adjusted* by these kinds of tax deductions.

Think about this for a second. Every dollar you put into your 401(k) gives you a discount on your federal income taxes (but not FICA taxes). For example, if you are in the 25 percent tax bracket, and you contribute $10,000, you have just lowered your taxes by $2,500! That's like a 25 percent rate of return on your money today that can grow tax-free until you take it out someday when it will be taxed, likely at a lower bracket.

Of course, many of us are actually paying way more than 25 percent, especially when we include state income taxes. We often pay taxes of 40 to 50 percent. That's an even higher discount on your money.

Second, at a minimum, *make sure to contribute at least up to the maximum match that your employer provides.* Your employer's dollar-for-dollar match is like an automatic 100 percent return. An employer's match of even 50 cents or 25 cents on the dollar is still like a 50 or 25 percent return, just for contributing.

Altogether, with a match, you may have just doubled your money by being tax efficient.

Lastly, get close to maxing out your contribution in order to lower both your federal and state income taxes. If you are under 50 years of age, the maximum you can put in your 401(k), as of 2014, is $17,500. If you are over 50 years of age, you can make an additional catch-up contribution of $5,500, for a total of $23,000.

2. Paycheck: Contribute to a 401(k) plus 457(b), or 403(b) plus 457(b)

Here's a huge point that many doctors miss out on. It is especially true that if you work for a hospital, you are likely to have *more* than one retirement plan.

You are very likely to have two or more retirement plans.

As you see, the IRS has a few weird quirks in the tax system.

Essentially, it boils down to this: you cannot contribute the maximum to both a 401(k) and a 403(b) (or SIMPLE IRA, SEP IRA, etc.). The most you can put between the two plans is the usual $17,500 plus catch-up provisions.

However, you can contribute $17,500 plus another $17,500 to a 401(k) or a 403(b), or a 457(b).

This is because 457(b)s are subject to completely different provisions under a separate part of the IRS code. Note that most employers *do not* make matching contributions to 457(b)s. So, you are better off first taking advantage of the 401(k) or 403(b).

However, as you pay off your debts and your discretionary income skyrockets, take advantage of this provision.

If you pay taxes of 50 percent between federal and state income taxes, you could easily save $17,500 in taxes by maxing out both plans every year.

Remember to pay yourself first!

3. Paycheck and Line 25 of IRS Form 1040: Contribute to a Health Savings Account

Yet another awesome way to take advantage of deductions before taxes is to fund money into a health savings account (HSA).

Contribution limits are significantly less than 401(k)/403(b)/457(b) limits: $3,300 for individuals; $6,550 for families, plus a $1,000 catch-up limit.

Normally, most folks pay for medical expenses like deductibles, co-pays, and co-insurance out of pocket. What is fantastic about an HSA is that you are paying an expense using money that has NEVER experienced federal or state income taxes. Additionally, when you take the money out for health-specific expenses, it comes out tax-free.

The beauty of HSAs is that they can roll over to the next year and year after that and the year after that if you don't use the money. This is a huge advantage over a cafeteria plan or other older plans where if you didn't use it, you lost it.

This means that you could save and save (if you aren't currently having any health issues) and have money stocked for medical expenses in retirement that you can withdraw tax-free in addition to being a tax deduction when you deposit the money in the HSA.

Definitely, max this out!

You can see this line on both your paycheck and, possibly, line 25 of IRS Form 1040 if you self-funded an HSA.

4. Line 12 of IRS Form 1040: Set Up a Business or Moonlight as a Consultant

The US tax code is set up to benefit one person: the business owner.

If you want to take advantage of the tax system and work its loopholes (legally), check out line 12 of IRS Form 1040 and Schedule C. There are many expenses that business owners can take advantage of.

I know that all of us are very busy and may not have a single extra second to dedicate to another money-making venture.

However, I strongly encourage you to start your own small business. Many people today sell trinkets or hobbies through eBay or Amazon.com. One of my friends worked for a Fortune 500 company as an analyst and yet found the time to "moonlight" selling mixed martial arts equipment on Amazon.com.

He is now making more money from the part-time business than from his full-time job and recently left his full-time job to go after the "part-time" gig.

What are your talents? What are your passions? What is something that wouldn't take a whole lot of time and has a low barrier to starting up?

Note that the IRS has some very specific guidelines regarding losses in a business: you must have the intent to make a profit. There are many ways that you can show this, including having your own website/Facebook page, showing revenue, having marketing and business plans, and much more.

I mentioned in the "Five Steps to Get Out of Debt" chapter that you should check out Nineline.com or FreelancePhysician.com for physicians' moonlighting opportunities. You can be paid $150/hour or more.

What opportunities could be available to you?

5. Use Business Owner Deductions

Have you considered setting up your own small business? Here are some points to consider:

- If you don't have the time, could your spouse start the business instead?

- What are your passions? What do you enjoy that could bring in money and give you some great tax deductions?

The following is an example of clients who started a business based upon their skills and interests:

Sam and Elizabeth recently retired. When they built their dream home, it was with the longstanding plan that Elizabeth would have an art studio in the home. For years, this plan had taken a backseat to Sam's career and raising the kids.

They added a separate studio, office, and classroom. During the week, Elizabeth teaches art, works on commercial graphic design, and creates original paintings to sell at local art fairs. They set up a limited liability corporation for the art business.

They were able to write off all costs related to the building and furnishing of the studio and office as well as the prorated share of their home utilities. They used IRS Section 179 of the tax code to expense up to $125,000 of their tangible personal property expenses for computers, and so on, each year.

They write off all materials and business advertising. They write off part of their automotive expenses. Lastly, they write off any other travel-related expenses in selling the art at fairs and exhibitions. The write-offs allow them to reduce Sam's income tax so their Social Security is not taxed. This led to a reduction of their overall tax percentage.

Their art business is beginning to make money. Elizabeth is happy painting and they are living their dream retirement while saving on income taxes along the way. Because their overall AGI dropped, they were able to write off a greater percentage of their other deductible expenses.

A couple of things to note here:

- You don't necessarily need to be the business owner; your spouse could play that role.
- There are many potential write-offs, including using a home office, which allows even more deductions. Listed below are several deductions worth considering:
    - Write off the costs of starting a business.
    - Use an IRS Section 179 deduction allowing you to expense tangible, personal property worth up to $125,000 per year.
    - Expense travel related to the business.
    - Take a home office deduction, as well as a part of your utilities.

- Write off part of your car if you use it for business.
- Buy something that you can write off for your business and that will improve your business income prospects while reducing income tax.
- Remodel a basement as a tax-deductible home office and deduct 100 percent of all costs related to the office.
- Buy a computer.
- Write off some of your insurance costs.
- Deduct interest related to the business.

RETIREMENT PLAN

What retirement plan do you have (401(k)/403(b)/SIMPLE IRA/etc.)?

- **Match.** Is it matched? How much is the match?

- **How much.** How much are you putting in your primary retirement plan annually?

- **Max it out.** Are you maxing out your plan? Are you over 50 years old? Are you taking advantage of the catch-up provision?

- **Second plan.** Do you have a second retirement plan—457(b)?

- **The catch-up.** How much are you putting in your secondary retirement plan annually? Are you over 50 years old? Are you taking advantage of the catch-up provision?

- **Owner only 401(k).** If you don't have any employees (e.g., as a consultant or small business owner), you should strongly consider an Owner Only 401(k)—also called Solo (k) and other similar names.

- **Defined benefit plan.** If you have the ability to sock away even more money, or you own your own practice, consider a defined benefit plan or a defined benefit plan with a carve-out. You can tax-deduct tens of thousands of dollars more than you can with a traditional plan such as a 401(k)/SIMPLE IRA. These plans are particularly beneficial to owners who are older than their employees or have only a few employees who have a short tenure.

Check out this story!

THE DEFINED BENEFIT PLAN

A client from Colorado had a lot of success in his professional field, but he was tired of the rat race.

He was burned out going through the grind, day after day after day. He was tired of working "for the man." So, he decided to join up with a colleague to start a business.

I was really excited for him but, honestly, a bit nervous. I've seen several small businesses flounder for a few years before making decent profitability.

But man, they really hit it out of the park! I was shocked at their jaw-dropping level of success.

In year one, they had over $1,000,000 in revenue, netting them over $500,000!

THE DEFINED BENEFIT PLAN (CONT.)

They were incredibly nervous about the taxes. Most of the earnings would have thrown them into incredibly high federal and state tax brackets of somewhere between 40 and 50 percent (not even including FICA taxes on W-2 wages).

That is a hell of a tax bill!

We spent a lot of time looking at different options including the SEP IRA, the SIMPLE IRA, and the traditional 401(k), but none of them could offer the deduction they were seeking.

I checked with a few resources and was pleasantly surprised to find out that new businesses can be eligible for defined benefit plans. I had previously thought that business owners had to have a track record of a few years.

We were able to set up a combination defined benefit and 401(k) plan. They were able to sock away over $200,000 of taxable income. This was a tax savings of over $80,000, the equivalent of buying a new Tesla!

And then, to top it all off, they could plan on doing it again the next year. I love it when we can make such a huge impact. It pumps me up!

Feel free to contact me with any questions about either of those plans. They can be very complex and you want to set them up correctly.

MANAGING CAPITAL GAINS AND DIVIDENDS

I have a basic philosophy in life: control the stuff that you can. Understand it. Learn about it to empower yourself with the best possible information to make quality decisions.

Unfortunately, we don't have power in many areas in our lives. Roll with the punches for the stuff that you cannot control. Keep it going and adjust as necessary.

Listen. We can't control what happens in an individual stock or security. Well, maybe Warren Buffet can. I suppose if I had a couple of billion dollars, I could drive up the price of a stock.

Yet, we've all seen people go broke or make really crappy financial decisions.

Here's the thing: you can control the capital gains and dividends when you own individual stocks and ETFs.

That's because you can sell them *at any time* during the business day. You can sell a position at a loss or at a gain. Nobody is going to force you to sell a position. Unfortunately, mutual funds are much more difficult to control. Let me explain.

Mutual funds can have "phantom capital gains." Essentially, mutual funds will distribute capital gains even when you haven't sold anything. Instead, the active manager buys and sells securities on your behalf. As assets come into the fund, they will be used to buy stocks or other securities.

When investors redeem their money, the fund manager will have to sell stocks or other securities.

This means that mutual funds are subject to the whims of investors, which can be bad news for tax efficiency. If you are invested in a "hot fund" that has capital gains from *unsold* positions that the manager bought years earlier (before you even invested in the fund), and investors start pulling their dough, you could be left with a big tax bill.

As a matter of fact, you could actually lose money in a mutual fund and still get caught with a capital gain distribution. Let me explain a case where this happened.

	2006	2007	2008	2009	2010	2011	2012	2013
Price (NAV)			10.31					
Short-term Cap Gain	0	0	1.3558	0	0	0	0	0
Long-term Cap. Game	0	0	2.9595	0	0	0	0	0
Gains as %			41.86%					

2006	2007	2008	2009	2010	2011	2012	2013
+25.98%	+43.72%	-61.27%	+75.14%	+17.19%	-21.39%	+0.49%	+8.19%

Consider the case of Ivy Global Natural Resources (ticker symbol: IGNYX). Here is the information on capital gains distributions from 2006 to 2013 (source: Morningstar.com):

If you invested on January 1, 2006, you would have been a very happy camper in 2006 and 2007. You would have been up 80 percent and more in two years. That's awesome.

But let's say that you held on to the fund through 2008. You would have *lost* 61.27 percent, and on top of that, because of all the share redemptions, you would have owed taxes, both short-term capital gains (taxed at ordinary income—yuck!) and long-term capital gains (taxed at favorable rates) for a total of 41.86 percent of your investment.

You might be down 30 percent overall since your initial investment would have had to be used to pay gains on an investment you didn't make. It's nuts!

However, it could be worse. You could be the poor shmuck who saw the track record in 2006 and 2007 and thought that this investment was a "sure bet" in 2008. If you had invested $100,000 in IGNYX on January, 1, 2008 and hadn't sold it by the end of the year, your investment would now be worth about $39,000, and on top of that, you would owe capital gains taxes on about $16,000 of that investment.

To add insult to injury, you would not have seen even a year of gains in the fund as did the relatively luckier person who invested on January 1, 2006 and experienced two great years.

Needless to say, you must be very careful about which mutual funds you invest in. Some managers are incredibly tax efficient, but you need to be sure they are tax efficient when you are investing nonqualified money.

Now, I'll step off that soap box and focus on more practical ways to help you with "tax harvesting."

TAX HARVESTING- TIS THE SEASON

The basic idea of tax harvesting is that you purposely create capital gains or capital losses.

> You must be very careful about which mutual funds you invest in... you need to be sure they are tax efficient when investing nonqualified money.

Let's go back a little. What showed on line 13 on your IRS Form 1040? Was there anything there? Was there a capital gain, a capital loss? If you had a capital loss, how much did you write off?

Did you have a carry-forward capital loss (line 13 of the Schedule D)?

If you had capital gains, here's the rub: the government has no ceiling on the amount it can tax you. You will get taxed on $3,000 of gain, $25,000 of gain, or even $100,000 of gain if you experience (realize) that gain.

On the other hand, unfortunately, the government does set a floor on the losses you can write off for capital losses. As a matter of fact, you can only write off $3,000 worth of losses per year. This is why people have carry-forward losses that roll over into the following year (or years!). It really ticks me off, frankly, but that's the way it is.

What you have to do is *manage* your capital gains by harvesting what you need.

For example, let's say it is November 30. You will want to explore your realized and unrealized gains/losses for the year to date.

Perhaps you have no carry-forward losses and, for the year, you have realized some capital gains. Review all of your nonqualified accounts to see if you have a position or two that may have been in the doldrums since you invested in it.

You may have some capital losses that you can harvest to offset the gains and even create a loss for the year while continuing to hold on to your winners.

That is tax efficiency, my friends, with you controlling what you can.

By the way, you will want to wait at least 31 days before buying back that sold security in order to avoid getting into trouble with the IRS and the SEC. They call it a "wash sale" if you buy back the stock sooner; that's illegal. Please don't do anything illegal.

Let's flip that scenario around. What if, instead, you do have carry-forward capital losses? You will want to harvest your capital gains.

I've seen people with $100,000 or even $200,000 worth of carry-forward losses. With a write-off of a mere $3,000 per year, it would take 33 years to write off $100,000.

Remember to be careful. It makes good sense to keep $10,000 to $15,000 of losses that you can write off in the foreseeable future.

Unlike losses, there are no regulations surrounding selling positions at a gain. The IRS doesn't care if you sell a position in one year and buy it back the next year.

Review your 2008, 2011, and last year's tax returns and Schedule D if you had capital gains or losses. Where did your gains and losses come from? Could your investments have been managed more tax efficiently? Did you have any mutual funds with phantom capital gains in 2008 or 2011? Make sure to eliminate the "ivy globals" of your portfolio.

BEING CHARITABLE

Among the best things I see clients do is giving to others. They give their time, energy, effort, and money to some great causes.

Maybe they give to their church or to their alma mater, to Big Brothers/Big Sisters or to a local theatre and arts program. I love seeing clients make an impact in their world!

Beyond your family, what are the important ways in which you would like to give back? What causes are you passionate about?

The awesome news is that you can get a tax deduction or even possibly avoid taxation by unleashing your giving spirit.

Under our current tax code, if your itemized deductions amount to more than the standard deduction, you can have a higher tax write-off than many Americans.

Keep in mind that your state income taxes and mortgage interest are currently counted toward your itemized deductions.

By adding some charitable giving to the mix, most of us can easily exceed the standard deduction limits and thus be able to itemize.

What makes charitable donations different from some other itemized deductions is that you don't have to exceed a certain percentage of your income.

> Payments to individuals are never deductible. For tax deductible gifts, you must maintain a record of the contribution with names, dates, and amounts. Noncash property requires an appraisal.

For example, in order to itemize medical expenses, your medical expenses have to exceed 7.5 percent of your AGI. Otherwise, you cannot itemize them.

In comparison, qualified charitable gifts can effect a substantial deduction from your income if you can itemize them. There's no minimum that you must donate. Just gift something and then some more and you will be helping your community and the world, as well as getting a tax write-off.

The IRS notes the following on its website. I have italicized the information that I thought was the most critical:

> To be deductible, charitable contributions must be made to qualified organizations. *Payments to individuals are never deductible.* See Publication 526, "Charitable Contributions." To determine if the organization that you have contributed to qualifies as a charitable organization for income tax deductions, review Exempt Organizations Select Check on the IRS.gov website.
>
> If your contribution entitles you to merchandise, goods, or services, including admission to a charity ball, banquet, theatrical performance, or sporting event, *you can deduct only the amount that exceeds the fair market value of the benefit received.*
>
> For a contribution of cash, check, or other monetary gift (regardless of amount), *you must maintain as a record of the contribution a bank record or a written communication from the qualified organization containing the name of the organization, the date of the contribution,*

and the amount of the contribution. In addition to deducting your cash contributions, you generally can deduct the fair market value of any other property you donate to qualified organizations. See Publication 561, "Determining the Value of Donated Property." *For any contribution of $250 or more* (including contributions of cash or property), you must obtain and keep in your records a contemporaneous written acknowledgment from the qualified organization indicating the amount of the cash and a description of any property contributed.

The acknowledgment must say whether the organization provided any goods or services in exchange for the gift and, if so, must provide a description and a good faith estimate of the value of those goods or services. One document from the qualified organization may satisfy both the written communication requirement for monetary gifts and the contemporaneous written acknowledgment requirement for all contributions of $250 or more.

You must fill out Form 8283 (PDF), and attach it to your return, if your deduction for a noncash contribution is more than $500. If you claim a deduction for a contribution of noncash property worth $5,000 or less, you must fill out Form 8283, Section A.

If you claim a deduction for a contribution of noncash property worth more than $5,000, you will need a qualified appraisal of the noncash property and must fill out Form 8283, Section B. If you claim a deduction for a contribution of noncash property worth more than $500,000, you also will need to attach the qualified appraisal to your return.

Special rules apply to donations of certain types of property such as automobiles, inventory, and investments that have appreciated in value. For more information, refer to Publication 526, "Charitable Contributions." For information on determining the value of your noncash contributions, refer to Publication 561, "Determining the Value of Donated Property."

Here are the main points from this document about charitable giving while getting a tax deduction:

1. Keep great records.

2. You can contribute with cash or a check.

3. You can also contribute property or an appreciated asset (but you may need to have a valuation done if it is over $5,000).

I cannot overstate the tremendous implications of having the ability to contribute an appreciated asset.

This means that if you have a position with a huge unrealized gain, you never have to realize it.

Instead, you can gift it (or part of it) to a charitable organization as is and receive a deduction for doing so.

The following are some other more specialized strategies that many doctors should consider as well.

FOUNDATIONS AND CHARITABLE REMAINDER TRUSTS

You can set up your own foundation or charitable remainder trust (CRT) and donate an appreciated asset *directly* to your foundation, or CRT, and get a tax write-off. In the case of the foundation, you can distribute a percentage of the foundation's funds to charities of your choice. Essentially, you are maintaining control of an asset and have a say in its growth, creating a legacy portfolio that your kids can continue to maintain after your passing and thus continue to make a difference in the world.

This is the exact strategy that Bill Gates has employed. It has allowed him to avoid paying hundreds of millions of dollars in capital gains.

Initially, the CRT is the same as a foundation in that you can contribute highly appreciated assets and get a tax write-off.

Then, you start an income stream back to yourself that is taxable (possibly, just partially). Whatever is left in the trust at your passing is contributed to the organizations of your choosing when you established the trust.

RMD STRATEGIES

Another charitable strategy that I think is far too under-utilized is charitable giving through required minimum distributions (RMDs).

Once you hit 70.5 years old (don't ask me why the half year is specified; it's the IRS), you have to start taking distributions from your IRA or 401(k) or 403(b) (unless you are still working for a given employer).

Many physicians have very substantial IRAs. As a matter of fact, I have several clients who are required to take $50,000 to $150,000 in distributions every year. These distributions are normally *entirely* taxable.

However, here's the good news: if you direct part of, or all of, that distribution to a charitable cause (a qualified entity, not a person), you will not have to pay taxes on that amount.

WHERE TO PLACE THE RMD

Again, by having your own entity such as a charitable foundation or CRT, you can have the funds gifted to the charities of your choice while having control over the investments and allowing them to continue to grow on your own terms over the years.

Make sure to review the tax law before you consider using this loophole. Congress has to approve it every year. As of the time of writing this guide (September 2014), this is still a strategy that you can employ.

REVIEW, REVIEW, REVIEW

Review your last year's tax return. Did you itemize your taxes or take the standard deduction? How close were you to being able to itemize your deductions?

Review Schedule A in your tax return. What itemized line items were you able to take advantage of?

How much did you give in charitable contributions? Could you do more and take advantage of the tax code?

Review your nonqualified accounts (money that is not in IRA accounts). Do you have positions with large capital gains?

Do you have need of this money? Could you establish your own foundation or CRT and take the tax write-off?

Are you nearly 70.5 years old, or older? Do you need all of your required minimum distribution? Could you donate some of it?

MORE DEDUCTIONS AND WRITE-OFFS

Beyond what I have already mentioned, there are a host of regular unreimbursed expenses that many physicians incur annually regardless of whether they are a small business owner or own their practice.

You want to make sure to look at each one of these to determine whether or not a deduction for unreimbursed expenses may apply to you.

Consider that some physicians are paid via W-2, meaning that they are employees of an organization, while other physicians are paid via 1099-MISC, meaning that they are independent contractors.

There are different rules that apply to each.

I've even met and worked with several physicians who are a combination of the two, particularly ER doctors who have seniority status.

MDTaxes.com does a wonderful job of summing up the data in a table on its website. Check it out! Here are a couple of snippets that I think are really worth mentioning:

- How you deduct your allowable unreimbursed professional expenses depends on how you were compensated during the year.

- Individuals compensated as employees (having taxes withheld from their pay) are required to deduct these type expenses as a miscellaneous itemized deduction on their Schedule A. These individuals are also required to complete and attach a Form 2106 or 2106-EZ, Unreimbursed Employee Business Expense, to their Form 1040.

- Individuals compensated as independent contractors (having no taxes withheld) deduct their professionals' expenses directly against their income. These individuals are required to complete and attach a Schedule C or Schedule C-EZ, Profit or Loss from Business, to their Form 1040.

- Individuals compensated as both employees and independent contractors need to determine whether to reflect a specific expense on the Schedule C or the Form 2106. Items which are specifically related to a person's income as an independent contractor, such as malpractice insurance and directly related auto expenses, will be deducted directly against that income. Other items, such as job search expenses, are most likely related to a person's employment and should be reflected on the Form 2106.

  IRS Pubs indicates the IRS Publication that contains information on this topic. You can access the IRS Pubs at www.irs.gov.

Review last year's tax return. Which unreimbursed expenses did you take advantage of?

Which expenses listed on MDTaxes.com might you be able to utilize in the future?

"BACK-DOOR" ROTH IRA

Way back in the early 2000s, as the Twin Towers toppled in New York, President Bush and a Republican Congress pushed through temporary tax incentives in order to get businesses to unleash their cash and to help consumers and individual investors to have more money to spend.

Because these measures were only meant to be temporary, we called this strategy the "sunsetting" of various provisions as they expired in 2010. Our split Congress could not agree on what to do in 2010, 2011, or 2012.

Capital gains taxes stayed low, estate tax exemption dropped, and the Roth IRA conversion limit moved from being capped at $100,000 of AGI to being unlimited.

Our crazy Congress went right to the brink, flirting with the idea of going into default on our debts. Essentially, the government was playing a game of chicken, seeing who would swerve off the road first.

Finally, at the very end of 2012, our government was done playing games (for now?) and came to a settlement. The result was that there were a number of provisions that changed with the fiscal cliff.

However, there are quite a few that have not, including Roth IRA conversions.

The purpose of this section is to do a quick overview of the traditional IRA compared with the Roth IRA and then let you in on the secret of putting money into a Roth IRA regardless of what your income tax bracket is if you are still employed.

Finally, we'll address some of the pitfalls and caveats of doing a Roth IRA conversion.

First, why put money in a traditional IRA or a Roth IRA?

It's all about trying to be as tax efficient as possible and keeping money out of Uncle Sam's hands, whether in the short term or long term. Traditional IRAs, 401(k)s, and 403(b)s are all focused on trying to do one thing: save money on taxes today.

In the case of the traditional IRA, if you fall within a given tax situation and you currently earn income from a job, you can make a contribution of which every last cent is tax deductible, and you can write off the contribution on your taxes.

FREEDOM FORMULA FOR PHYSICIANS

However, by getting a tax deduction today, you are waiting to pay federal/state income taxes on those funds until you withdraw that money.

Below is a table showing where your income would need to be in order for this to happen.

Meanwhile, Roth IRAs are focused on saving money on taxes later.

The basic concept is that you have already paid taxes on the money and so when you withdraw the money after reaching the age of 60, you don't have to pay any taxes on the money you invested in the Roth IRA or on the growth of that money.

Check out the table to see where your income would need to be in order to contribute to a Roth IRA.

IRA DEDUCTION IF YOU ARE COVERED BY A RETIREMENT PLAN AT WORK AS OF 2014

If your filig status is...	and your modified AGI is...	then you can take ...
single or head of household	$60,000 or less	$5,500 if under 50 $6,500 if over 50
	more than $60,000 but less than $70,000	a partial deduction
	$70,000 or more	no deduction
married filing jointly or qualifying widow (er)	$96,000 or less	$5,500 if under 50 $6,500 if over 50
	more than $96,000 but less than $116,000	a partial deduction
	$116,000 or more	no deduction
married filing seperately	leass than $10,000	a partial deduction
	$10,000 or more	no deduction

ROTH IRA CONTRIBUTION LIMITS

If your filing status ia...	and your modified AGI is...	then you can contibuite...
married filing jointly or qualifying widow (er)	<$181,000	$5,500 if under 50 $6,500 if over 50
	≥$181,000 but <$191,000	a reduced amount
	≥$191,000	zero
married filing seperately and you living with your spouse at any time during the year	<$10,000	a reduced amount
	>$10,000	zero
Single, head of household, or married filing seperately and you did not live with your spouse at any time during the year	<$114,000	$5,500 if under 50 $6,500 if over 50
	≥$114,000 but <$129,000	a reduced amount
	≥$129,000	zero

However, this is where things start to get interesting.

What if your AGI is over $191,000? You'd look at this table and think, "Man! I can't make an IRA contribution or a Roth IRA contribution!"

Guess what? Like many other things with the government, there are certain caveats to be aware of.

What you can do is contribute to a nondeductible IRA in which you don't get a tax deduction and there is no income restriction for putting money in, but then, no matter your income, you can convert those funds from the nondeductible IRA to a Roth IRA.

Back in 2010 when a bunch of tax incentives began to sunset, part of the package was to lift the cap off Roth IRA conversions.

Prior to 2010, if you were married and your income was over $100,000, you couldn't convert to a Roth IRA. However, since then, there is no income restriction!

This provision continued in 2011, 2012, 2013, and 2014.

The bottom line here is that through a bit of paperwork shuffling and moving assets around, no matter your income, you have the ability to contribute to a Roth IRA.

It's crazy! I don't know why they don't just lift the income cap off the Roth IRA. I guess that's the insanity of government for you.

This is a fantastic financial planning tool, but I do want to point out a couple of pitfalls.

- First, make sure that your nondeductible IRA contribution is set up in a completely separate account from any deductible IRA money. If you mix the two together, it can become a paperwork nightmare to track.

- Second, the best possible scenario for a straightforward conversion is to have no traditional tax-deductible IRA money at all, as, for example, with 401(k)s, 403(b)s, and 457(b)s. However, if you convert traditional tax-deductible IRA funds to a Roth IRA, the transaction is taxable.

- Disclaimer: It may not be beneficial to convert in all cases, particularly when there is taxable money involved. You're essentially betting that your tax rate will be higher in retirement than it is now. You are choosing to pay that cost now rather than later. Note that it may take five years or longer for this to be beneficial.

- Third, you want to *immediately* convert (assuming there will be no tax consequences from other IRA money) to a Roth IRA. You do not want to have earnings on the nondeductible IRA. This could lead to additional taxes when you do convert.

- Fourth, spouses can be treated differently. If one spouse has a significant amount of traditional tax-deductible IRA money and the other spouse has no tax-deductible IRA money, the spouse without tax-deductible IRA money should contribute to a nondeductible IRA and then contribute to a Roth IRA. You want to avoid utilizing the spouse with IRA money when you have a choice.

Let me show you two examples (for illustrative purposes only):

EXAMPLE ONE

John has $100,000 in a traditional tax-deductible IRA, $100,000 in his 401(k), and $5,000 that he contributed to a nondeductible IRA. If he wants to convert the $5,000 nondeductible to a Roth IRA, he can only move over part of it as nontaxable. The majority would be taxed.

How does he figure this out?

He ignores the $100,000 in 401(k) money; it doesn't count. He adds up the $100,000 in the tax-deductible IRA, plus the $5,000 in the nondeductible IRA, which gives him a total of $105,000. The $5,000 is divided by $105,000, which comes to 4.8 percent. So, more than 95 percent of this conversion would be taxed. Of the nondeductible $5,000, he'd only move about $250 to a Roth IRA.

Not a great situation. John probably wouldn't want to go through the hassle of this process.

EXAMPLE TWO

John has $2,000 in a traditional tax-deductible IRA, $100,000 in his 401(k), and $5,000 that he contributed to a nondeductible IRA. If he wants to convert the $5,000 nondeductible amount to a Roth IRA, he can contribute almost all of it as nontaxable and next year, assuming the same rules apply, contribute even more.

Once again, he ignores the $100,000 in 401(k) money; it doesn't count. He adds the $2,000 in the tax-deductible IRA to the $5,000 in the nondeductible IRA, which gives him a total of $7,000. The amount of $5,000, divided by $7,000 comes to 71.4 percent.

So, less than 30 percent of this conversion would be taxed. Of the nondeductible $5,000, he'd move about $3,500 to a Roth IRA without it being taxed. He'd also move $1,500 of the tax-deductible account to a Roth IRA, which would be taxed.

Of course, the best situation is having no tax-deductible IRA money, because then you can convert 100 percent.

 BIG IDEA: Conversions are done on an individual basis. The tax-free conversion could focus on the spouse with NO deductible IRA money.

However, given the example we showed above, within a couple of years, by pro-rata converting the non-deductible IRA and a relatively small, deductible IRA account (think $10,000 or less) could work just as well because the tax consequences and the deductible IRA whittles down to nothing within a couple of years.

Then, you are scott-free to just do the non-deductible IRA contributions and conversion with ease.

Note that this is done on an individual basis. In the case of married couples, one spouse could have a bunch of deductible IRA money while the other has none. The tax-free conversion could focus on the spouse with no deductible IRA money.

Lastly, make sure you file the right tax forms when going through this process. For the Roth IRA conversion, you will receive a Form 1099 from your brokerage company, which will say that it is a taxable transaction. In order to get this corrected, you'll want to file Form 8606 for nondeductible IRAs, which tracks the calculations we described in our previous examples.

Let me briefly describe what you'll want to check off (assuming your tax bracket disqualifies you for a deduction):

- ✔ List and confirm that you contributed to a traditional IRA.

- ✔ You did not switch or re-characterize the contribution.

- ✔ You made and tracked nondeductible contributions to your IRA.

- ✔ Your IRA deduction should be zero.

- ✔ You should have received a 1099R form from your broker/ clearing firm.

- ✔ Important: Your 1099 may show a taxable distribution and taxable amount of same amount, but the taxable amount not determined should be checked off.

- ✔ You then note that you moved the money to another retirement account and converted the money to a Roth IRA

- ✔ Your double check is line 15b, which should be zero if you immediately converted with no earnings.

Do either you or your spouse have money in a traditional tax-deductible IRA?

If making the back-door Roth, make sure to use the spouse with the least amount of traditional tax-deductible IRA for the transaction.

Remember, the amounts in 401(k)s, 457(b)s, and 403(b)s do not count in the Roth conversion.

Traditional IRAs are great because you have the whole world of investments available to you rather than being constrained to solely the choices in the "menu" that your employer provides.

However, if that isn't important to you consider moving the traditional tax-deductible IRA to your current employer-sponsored plan so that next year you can take full advantage of the back-door Roth.

Disclaimer: Please note that this should not be taken as specific investment or tax advice and you should consult a professional before deciding whether a conversion may be right for you.

Alright, so we have spent lots and lots of time on tax strategies. You've encountered some great concepts that you're not likely to see in many other places.

CHAPTER SUMMARY

There are many different kinds of taxes: income taxes, property taxes, sales taxes, business and occupation taxes, and much more.

We focused on three kinds of taxes: income taxes, payroll taxes, and capital gains taxes for individuals.

Income taxes can be imposed by the federal government and state government Both the federal and state income tax systems are tiered, bracketed systems. This means the more money you make, the higher the percentage in taxes you pay as you move up the tax brackets.

The great news here is that this is the easiest kind of tax to be proactive with. Here's how it works:

Assuming you are married, your tax bracket does not change for the first $18,150 of your income.

It does change for the additional amount of income above $18,500. If you had an income of $20,000, you would be taxed $1,815 for the first $18,150 of it, plus 15 percent on the remainder of your total income ($1,850), or $277.50, for a grand total of $2,092.50.

Your income is currently in the 15 percent bracket, but your effective tax rate is 10.46 percent. This is the difference between tax bracket and tax rate.

Capital gains taxes are the taxes paid on investments after they have been sold at a profit. This can occur in real estate, stocks, bonds, small businesses, and much more.

There are two different types of capital gains taxes: long-term and short-term. Short-term capital gains are incurred when you buy and sell an asset within a year. Long-term capital gains occur when you hold an asset for longer than a year.

Meanwhile, payroll taxes are the social program taxes that support Social Security, Medicare, and Medicaid.

Without a doubt, payroll taxes are the hardest taxes to avoid. There are no standard deductions, itemized deductions or credits that can offset payroll taxes. They are pretty much out of your control unless you own a clinic in a small partnership, or you are a sole proprietor.

What is completely different about payroll taxes is that they are paid by both the employer and the employee

There are five basic ways to reduce your taxable income without taking a pay cut. First, contribute to your primary retirement plan. Second, see if you have a 457(b) plan or another deferred compensation plan and max that out. Third, contribute to a health savings account. Fourth, be a business owner. Fifth, use the loads of tax deductions that being a business owner affords you.

Capital gains are completely in your control. Look to harvest losses or gains in order to maximize your tax situation. Watch out for phantom gains from mutual funds.

Give back to your community and causes important to you through charitable giving. Consider utilizing your own foundation as Bill Gates does as a way to avoid taxation on appreciated assets or large required minimum distributions.

Lastly, consider utilizing a "back-door" Roth IRA. Make sure to carefully review your situation. If you are married, it may be better to utilize your spouse if you have a significant amount of traditional IRA money and your spouse does not. Make sure to file the right tax forms.

RESOURCES

If you would like to take part in a free webinar, make sure to check out my website at www.daviddenniston.com/tax-webinar.

Also, check out my workbook on the subject: *The Tax Reduction Prescription Workbook: 6 Secrets to Reducing Taxes for Doctors*—with specific exercises and templates for you to complete. It is for sale on Amazon.com.

MDTaxes.com

FreeLancePhysician.com

CHAPTER 4

INVESTING 201: THE ADVANCED COURSE ON INVESTMENTS

The next step is to help you explore the vast world of investments.

Back in medical school and residency, you were so busy with clinical trials, rotations, and your medical studies that they neglected to give you a course on investments.

How familiar are you with investments?

In my other book, *The Freedom Formula for Young Physicians*, I give an investing 101 course in which I talk about the difference between stocks and bonds, international and domestic investments, ETFs and mutual funds, and more.

This chapter is designed as "investing 201," an advanced course for those who are familiar with basic investing principles and want to understand the philosophy of a successful financial advisor who prides himself in his research.

If you would like to know more about the basics of investing, make sure to check out my website at daviddenniston.com, or contact me to purchase a copy of *The Freedom Formula for Young Physicians*.

For the rest of you, we'll start out with a brief review and then we'll dig into some of my latest research to give you some fantastic tools that I use every day for my clients.

In this chapter, we are going to address the following topics:

- Asset Allocation and Risk Tolerance
- Learning Lessons from History
- The January Effect
- The Best Technical Indicator
- Annuities: Shining Savior or Dastardly Villain?
- How to Generate Income from Annuities

ASSET ALLOCATION AND RISK TOLERANCE

First, what in the world is asset allocation? What does this mean?

To sum it up in a few words: Asset allocation is the way that you select your investments.

Asset allocation is designed to match different kinds of investments to help diversify your investments.

Think of the investment world as a big Asian buffet. You could get the salad bar, wonton soup, sautéed veggies, dumplings, fried rice, tempura, sushi, sweet and sour pork, kung pao chicken, and lots of other dishes. (I'm getting hungry!)

Some people have preferences for veggies and sushi while others prefer fried rice and dumplings. Everyone has different tastes, just as everyone pursues different objectives and goals.

There isn't any one asset allocation that fits all people.

Reflect on these questions for a little bit:

- Are you invested into stocks or bonds?

- How much do you have in stocks relative to bonds?

- Are your investments here in the United States or are they international investments?

- How much do you have in US investments relative to international investments?

- Are they older companies or newer companies?

- How much risk are you taking with your principal? What risks are you subject to?

- How can you protect yourself against some of these risks?

This may feel a bit overwhelming.

The first step that most folks need to take is completing a risk tolerance questionnaire.

This is a helpful initial determinant. Most risk tolerance questionnaires will ask questions about your time horizon, how much of a loss you can tolerate, and what your outlook is for investments and the economy.

I usually think of risk on a scale of one to five, with one being the most conservative and five being the most aggressive.

I usually think of moderate risk tolerance as a three, smack dab in the middle.

And, as they say in those infomercials, "but that's not all!"

Financial advisors will also take into consideration your goals and when you want to accomplish them. This can vary by client or even by the type of account.

For example, let's say you have a kiddo going off to college next year and you are going to be needing $50,000 out of the $100,000 you have invested in a joint account.

Your risk tolerance may likely be fairly conservative for the account you want to withdraw this from, even though you may not be retiring for another 10 years.

With this scenario, you may have a completely different risk tolerance in your retirement accounts than in your joint account because you're not going to need the money any time soon.

Another common scenario in which risk tolerance may need to be tweaked occurs when a client holds a lot of the employer's stock.

Some of my clients hold MMM and Microsoft stock that they get through stock awards and options. The stocks can be worth tens of thousands or even hundreds of thousands of dollars. We may need to be more cautious with their brokerage accounts due to this risk exposure.

Beyond these basic concepts, consider how actively you want your assets managed.

Would you rather have your advisor be proactive, adjusting the risk exposures regularly or, instead, every once in a while?

STRATEGIC VERSUS TACTICAL

To fit either of these situations, there are two types of asset allocation that most advisors focus on: strategic asset allocation and tactical asset allocation.

STRATEGIC ALLOCATION

Strategic asset allocation doesn't change very much; it is fairly static. For example, an investor with a moderate risk tolerance may have a mix of 60 percent stocks to 40 percent bonds. The advisor may change a manager here and there, but the mix of stocks to bonds doesn't change very often unless the risk tolerance of the client changes.

For the purposes of this discussion, I am assuming "alternative" asset classes such as precious metals, commodities, real estate, shorting the stock market and volatility investments are considered the equivalent of stocks, or riskier asset classes, as I like to call them.

TACTICAL ALLOCATION

Tactical asset allocation can change very frequently. Managers try to be proactive in managing one risk or another. For example, managers may be concerned about interest rates going up, so they may shift from long-term bonds to short-term bonds or to stocks.

Alternatively, managers may be more concerned about a recession and put more money in US Treasury bonds or other investments that are perceived to be safer, and less money in stocks.

So, now that you know all this lovely information, how do you apply it?

Let's say that you are looking through your 401(k) choices and you have a menu of choices. You see some performance data but don't know a whole lot about the investment options. You can't tell what kind of investments they are.

I may be a little biased, just a little, but I do think talking to an investment professional may help you evaluate your options.

However, if you would rather do it on your own, first find out your risk tolerance. There are tons of tools online to do that. Evaluate your goals and objectives, particularly with respect to your time frame.

After you have all this figured out, one major resource I point folks toward is Morningstar.com.

LOOK IT UP

You can look up practically any mutual fund or widely traded security. Categorize each of these investments and understand on a scale of 1 to 5 how volatile they can be.

- How did your investments perform in the downturn that started in late 2007 and continued through early 2009?

- Consider how they did in the recovery that started in March 2009 and continued through 2014.

If they went way down in the downturn and then way up in the upturn, you may have a volatile investment and vice versa if the ride was smoother.

THE RULE

My general rule of thumb is never to have more than 20 percent in any one investment (nor less than 5 percent in any one investment). Each investment should have a completely different objective and be subject to changes in value for different reasons. For example, emerging markets stocks will rise and fall in value for reasons that are different from the reasons that large cap US stocks change in value.

COMPARISONS

Those two asset classes move in value for a reason that is completely different from the reason that US Treasury bonds move up and down in value, and the value of US Treasury bonds changes for a different reason from the reason investment grade bonds change in value.

Additionally, be careful in your selection of bonds, as some bonds are more sensitive to changes in the economy than others.

For example, junk-rated or hi-yield companies are considered a poorer credit risk (meaning, they are more likely to go bankrupt) than investment grade companies, and can be more volatile. Sometimes, in periods of higher risk, they can act more like a hi-yield stock than a bond.

How does this work in practice? I suggest a mix of international and domestic investments, and after an evaluation, I may suggest a mix of international and domestic investments to accommodate both conservative and moderately aggressive risk tolerances.

Hopefully, you have a choice of international bond and stock investments as well as domestic investments.

Let's focus on one example. Let's say you are a conservative investor.

I'd suggest selecting less volatile investments with a smattering of more volatile investments. A typical mix of strategic asset allocation for a conservative investor is 40 percent equities to 60 percent bonds.

Aim for at least 25 percent of the total mix having an international component of developed and/or emerging markets within stocks and bonds.

Also, if you want to dabble and be a little crazy, consider having at least 10 percent of the total asset allocation mix in such "alternatives" as we mentioned before: precious metals, commodities, real estate, and so on, but they should account for no more than 10 percent of your portfolio.

Keep in mind this is only one example. Make sure you understand your risk tolerance, investment objective, and individual financial situation before making any investment decisions.

To get back to our earlier discussion of strategic asset allocation compared with tactical asset allocation: How do you decide what is right for you?

From my work with over 100 different clients, I have found that both can work and be very effective.

However, most folks I work with can't take the emotional roller coaster.

Strategic asset allocation—buy, hold, and rebalance—means investors have to cling on, bare knuckles, white in the face, as they swallow the losses that inevitably will happen from time to time.

Most folks love making money and climbing, climbing, and climbing to the top. But then they hate the ride down. They can't stand the thought of losing much of their hard-earned money.

They don't watch the market from day to day or even month to month, but they do open up their statements, and if they see a "big drop," their stomachs churn and churn from the ride, and they want to get off at the worst possible time.

Thus, I prefer tactical asset allocation for the majority of our clients.

While not perfect, it does work to minimize the downside risk and smooth the ride.

Many strategic asset allocators point out that you cannot perfectly time the market. They are absolutely right.

I can understand that sentiment, and here's the method behind my madness of how tactical asset allocation can and should work.

LEARNING LESSONS FROM HISTORY

In case you didn't know, I am a history buff. I love reading and learning about history.

Channel H2 is currently my favorite since the History channel is now all about reality shows and doesn't show any actual history.

If I were not a financial advisor, I would likely be a doctor or a history professor.

If you feel similarly, check out Ron Chernow. He does some fantastic biographies. I particularly recommend the ones on George Washington and Alexander Hamilton.

I digress.

I constantly seek to improve my skills, as a financial advisor, reading new materials and picking up time-tested strategies that I can research myself to double-check the data.

My ultimate goal is to help to protect clients on the downside, while still participating in the upside.

In 2012 I did some research, going back about 15 years, that I shared in my 2013 and 2014 *Year Looking Forward* newsletters.

I was struck by the fact that at some point every year there was a drop from January 1, even if ever so small. I have updated the table below.

Note that this reflects only the closing price, not intraday activity; it does not include dividends.

How can I learn from history to be as effective as I can be as an asset manager? Here is a summary of the data:

1. Fourteen out of 16 times (87.5 percent of the time), the S&P 500 index has been below its price from the beginning of the year.

2. Six times out of 16 (37.5 percent of the time), the low point has been a 10 percent drop or greater from the price at beginning of the year.

3. Twelve times out of 16 (75 percent of the time), the low point has been a 3 percent drop or greater from the price at the beginning of the year.

4. Five out of the last 16 calendar years end in a negative drop for the market (31 percent of the time), which is close to one out of every three years.

Check out the table below for all the details.

Year	Low Point %	High Point %	Year %
2013	0.00%	29.69%	29.69%
2012	0.00%	17.32%	13.47%
2011	-12.58%	8.49%	-0.20%
2010	-8.29%	14.01%	12.84%
2009	-24.10%	25.59%	23.49%
2008	-48.40%	0.00%	-38.28%
2007	-3.02%	10.49%	3.24%
2006	-1.58%	14.95%	13.74%
2005	-5.85%	5.74%	3.01%
2004	-3.98%	9.06%	8.62%
2003	-8.74%	26.07%	26.12%
2002	-31.67%	2.90%	-22.81%
2001	-25.84%	5.15%	-12.87%
2000	-13.98%	4.63%	-10.62%
1999	-1.69%	17.95%	19.03%
1998	-4.89%	28.08%	27.05%

Data derived from VectorVest and Standard and Poor's

In 2013, I decided to expand my research. Was 2012 an aberration in which there was no low point? How often has this been repeated in history?

Using the *Stock Trader's Almanac* by Hirsch, 2013 edition, we were able to pull up data all the way from 1930 to 1997 to fill in the blanks.

I am not going to publish all of the tables here, but I can make them available upon request. Here are the results:

1. Fifty-nine times out of 66 (89 percent of the time), the S&P 500 index has been below its price from the beginning of the year.

2. Twenty-eight times out of 66 (42 percent of the time), the low point has been a 10 percent drop or greater from the price at the beginning of the year.

3. Thirty-seven times out of 66 (56 percent of the time), the low point has been a 5 percent drop or greater from the price at the beginning of the year.

4. Forty-one times out of 66 (62 percent of the time), the low point has been a 3 percent drop or greater from the price at the beginning of the year.

5. Twenty-one out of 66 calendar years end in a negative drop for the market (31.8 percent of the time), which is close to one out of every three years.

CONCLUSIONS

Here are the conclusions I would pull from all of this data:

- First, a year when the market never turned down is not an aberration. It happens about 10 percent of the time, whether in recent history or in the distant past. I believe this means we always need to have some money invested in stocks, because there may never be a dip from the beginning of the year. However, a dip, even if ever so small, is extremely likely to happen on an annual basis.

- Second, if we hold a fairly conservative allocation with only 15 to 25 percent of investments in stocks, we should think about adding more to domestic stocks when the market drops by 3 percent or more. At a probability of about 62 to 75 percent, there is a very good (or perhaps extremely likely) chance of this happening on an annual basis.

- Third, we should expect about one out of every three years to end in the negative and about 40 percent of the time, we should expect a drop sometime during the year of 10 percent or greater from the price at the start of the year. However, since that is less than most of the time, you cannot wait and wait and wait in any given year for a large double-digit drop. You could easily miss out on some tremendous upside.

But how can you prepare for these drops that inevitably will happen and can be extremely painful?

After all, don't we want to buy low and sell high? This data isn't enough. It is good and helpful, especially in considering when to deploy new cash, but it doesn't help us to know when we need to be more conservative.

I challenged myself to dig deeper and see what trends I could find.

This led me to the January effect.

THE JANUARY EFFECT

I was first made aware of the January effect of the S&P 500 in *Stock Trader's Almanac*, but I frankly didn't pay much attention to it. For me, it was just some market timing gobbledy-gook.

However, after going through multiple up-and-down cycles. I figured there had to be a better way.

As I reviewed the January effect again in 2012 and 2013 and really took time to do my own research, I was shocked by the powerful results.

At first the data can be really overwhelming; there are more than 80 years of data to pore over!

Once you sort the S&P 500 by descending Januarys, starting in 1950, a pattern emerges like a powerful light from a lighthouse, cutting through the dense fog, showing the way to the coast.

First, we look at the starting price of the year, the low price of the year, the high price of the year, and the ending price for the year. Then, we calculate the percentage gains.

All you have to do is divide the years into three separate categories: Januaries of 4 percent or greater, Januaries of 0 to 3.99 percent, and negative Januaries.

January Effect	Number of Years	Low Point %	High Point %	Year Ending %
4% or >	19	-1.6%	25.9%	22.4%
0%-3.99%	20	-5.14%	15.22%	11.22%
Negative	24	-17.19%	6.6%	-4.01%

This is amazing stuff! Can you see the patterns?

THE BEST POSSIBLE JANUARY

First, when you have a January of 4 percent or better, the average year ends at 22 percent and the low point is a mere -1.6 percent.

What this table doesn't tell you is that nearly all of the years without a dip have a January of 4 percent. This happened recently in 2012 and 2013.

Out of the 11 occurrences since 1950, nine happened in a January of 4 percent. That is nearly half of the 19 Januaries of 4 percent!

Thus, when a January is a positive 4 percent, you *must* invest. And you cannot just partially invest. You must be fully invested via your risk tolerance. You cannot wait. Otherwise, you could miss out on an average additional gain of 18 percent.

Well, you may ask if some outliers significantly throw off the average. The answer, amazingly, is no.

Of the total 19 years, 14 years ended with a return of 18 percent. That means 73.68 percent of Positive 4% or greater Januaries had a very high double-digit return! That's a huge percentage.

Additionally, out of the 19 years total, 18 years ended with a positive, spread over the 4 percent January. That means that they ended at least 1 percent more or much higher from the beginning of the year. That's 95 percent of all of them; it's nuts!

THE SLIGHTLY POSITIVE JANUARY

Next, in a slightly positive January of 0 to 3.99 percent, we can see that results are still very positive, but not as stellar as a 4 percent January in which momentum was in full effect.

Notice the average year still ends at an amazing 11 percent, with an average positive January of 1.97 percent, or a spread of over 9 percent gain! That's 9 percent more of a gain after starting with a 2 percent gain.

Again, the average is not thrown off by many outliers. Fifteen out of 20 years end up at 7 percent or greater, which means 75 percent have a positive spread of 5 percent or more. However, this is where a -3 percent dip becomes commonplace. The average low point is -5.14 percent.

This begs the question of when you should put money to work. Should you wait for a double-digit dip? How common is that?

It does happen. Three years out of 20 years, or about 15 percent, have a low point of a double-digit dip. In my opinion, this does warrant review, but we cannot wait for it.

I would suggest a slightly positive January justifies putting most of your money, if not all of it, to work in a traditional asset allocation model.

If you do wait for a slight dip, that's okay. But don't wait too long and don't wait for a large dip because, a huge percentage of the time, it will never happen.

I will address in the next section how to identify and prepare for the big dip for the 15 percent scenario.

THE EPICALLY HORRIBLE JANUARY (OR NOT)

Lastly, let's address a negative January.

Talk about wow!

The average year that starts with a negative January ends with -4 percent and the average low point is -17 percent.

Ouch!

Not only that, but the average high point is only about 6 percent.

The numbers are powerful and very telling for the low point. Seventeen years out of 26 years, or 65 percent, have a double-digit dip. That is a powerful majority!

However, the remaining 35 percent have a low point of -5 to -9.99 percent.

Heck, 26 years out of 26 years have a -5 percent dip or more and have a spread from January—that is, all of them, 100 percent of them, have a lower low point than the low point at the end of January.

However, by the end of the year, the outliers can be slightly deceiving. Ten of the 26 years end positively, which is about 38 percent. Of those 10, only four end with positive double digits.

This is the mirror of the slightly positive January. You can still end the year in the positive, but great appreciation is not very likely (yet still slightly possible).

All in all, the big ugly is extremely likely (but not guaranteed) to occur after a negative January. This certainly makes it worth your while to strongly consider waiting for a dip.

However, once the S&P 500 dips to a slight negative, -5 percent or -6 percent, make sure to start putting money to work. Don't wait entirely for the big ugly. Otherwise, you could miss out on a positive year, which happens with frequency, even with a negative January.

As of the time of this writing, September 2014, this is exactly what happened this year.

So, the January effect is awesome and yet it isn't quite enough.

Let's chat about another tool in our tool bag that, when combined with the January effect, is a crazy, crazy, powerful combination.

Can you tell I'm excited? I love this stuff!

THE BEST TECHNICAL INDICATOR

A quick refresher course if you are relatively new to investing: There are two schools of thought in analyzing individual securities such as stocks—namely, <u>fundamental analysis and technical analysis.</u>

Fundamental analysis is all about the accounting statements—income statement, balance sheet, and the cash flow—and different ways to measure value from those statements, such as price-to-earnings ratios, dividend discount models, book value, profit growth, free cash flow, and so on.

Technical analysis is all about charts and trends. You see all these cool squiggly lines and bars. It can seem mystical, like reading tea leaves. Look at that chart! I can tell you exactly what is going to happen, based on this line or that, or this line plus that line.

Honestly, I used to be more of a fundamental analyst. I loved all the number crunching and the evaluation of a stock based on its accounting statements. Then, I came to realize, after Enron and Worldcom and others, that all of these numbers could be manipulated way too easily.

I was really skeptical of technical analysis.

Then, my partner Brett Machtig suggested the book *The Ivy Portfolio*, which discusses how the endowment funds of the Ivy League schools are run. Did you know that the endowment funds of Harvard, Yale, and other Ivy League schools use technical analysis to hedge against downside risk?

I was really surprised and shocked. Why would they use technical analysis? They must have an army of people looking over this data to make it work for them.

With my eyes open, I was willing to try it out. The book stated that the most frequently used technical tool is the 200-day moving average.

So, I decided to give it a whirl and crunched some numbers. Why not give it a try and see what happens?

Since that time, I have reviewed and tested over 30 different criteria.

I boiled down the extensive list to the two primary drivers: a long-term technical indicator, the 200-day moving average of the S&P 500, and long-term price points, the five-year high and low for the S&P 500.

BIG IDEA: Did you know that endowment funds of Ivy League schools use technical analysis to hedge against downside risk? The 200 day moving average is the most frequently used tool for those organizations.

I'm not going to tell you all the secrets of applying this stuff. It would take too long, but I do want you to understand the beauty of the system, and I think if you want to do it yourself, there are many lessons that you can apply.

Okay, why use the 200-day moving average?

It is a long-term directional trend.

Let me make this abundantly clear: I do not believe in day trading and short-term technical trends that many of those trendy software infomercials claim are the best thing since sliced bread.

They are attempting to take advantage of extremely short-term trends. They will look at the 25-day moving average, the 10-day moving average, and the 5-day moving average.

WHY NOT SHORT-TERM TRADING?

Guess what happens? The moving average crosses over the line again and again and again and again. You'll be trading so frequently your head will be spinning.

I can't keep track of that stuff and don't have the energy to do so.

And you can't always get it right. Keep in mind, no matter the theory, you will never sell at the very, very top, nor will you buy at the very, very bottom.

No theory will "perfectly" teach you how to do that.

However, by properly applying the 200-day moving average, you can participate in the biggest part of a multiyear upside trend and miss a huge part of the downside in a really cruddy year or year and a half.

The 200-day moving average has the advantage that you can make an unemotional decision.

If the price of the S&P 500 is *below* the 200-day moving average, the trend is negative. You want to have a lower stock exposure.

If the price of the S&P 500 is *above* the 200-day moving average, the trend is positive. You want to have more stock exposure.

The S&P 500 doesn't know about geopolitical risks such as Russia invading Ukraine, or a new world war brewing. It doesn't know about the number of unemployed or underemployed. It doesn't know about my job being sucky or my boss yelling at me. It doesn't know about my brother's friend's friend's stock tip.

Heck, it doesn't even know about the January effect.

It simply tells me about momentum. Is the long-term direction heading up or down?

It works wonderfully in long-term trending markets, which is the huge majority of the time.

On the next couple of pages, I have a couple of graphs of SPY, the exchange traded fund (ETF) that tracks the S&P 500, to illustrate how this would work.

First, there is a very long-term view of SPY from 2000 through 2013.

I've circled most of the spots where the 200-day moving average crosses the price line of SPY over 14 years.

On average, it occurs about once per year. Although, in times of big momentum, it may only occur every two or three years.

Check it out! See how we can avoid day trading and still use technical analysis to avoid the downside.

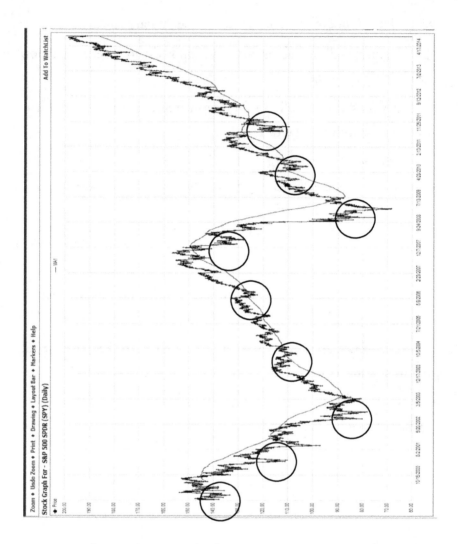

Now that you've seen the long-term trend, let me highlight a few other examples for you.

Source: VectorVest

This is a chart from 2012. Note how there was a bounce below the less choppy line, the 200-day moving average, but then it bounced right back.

By simply watching the long-term trend of the 200-day moving average, you aren't moving in and out every day, every week, or even every month, but, maybe, once a year or less.

Source: VectorVest

This is a chart showing December 2006 to December 2008. Note how the more volatile price line breached the smooth line of the 200-day moving average and didn't recover until years later.

Thus, if the market continues to rise with a bump or two along the way, we will participate in it throughout the year.

The risk happens when the S&P doesn't rise much and then falls a little bit and then rises a little and then falls a little bit and then rises a little bit.

Imagine it looking like a steady electrocardiogram (EKG). That is great in medicine but horrible in technical analysis. It does happen but not very often.

Most of the time, the market trends either up or down.

Nonetheless, the following chart shows a period when the 200-day moving average did not work very well.

This very brief period in late 2007 is the worst-case scenario for the technical indicator, which is up 6 percent and then down 6 percent, oscillating around the 200-day moving average.

Note that it was very short-term—two months in total.

In the name of full disclosure, it can happen and I expect it will happen again.

However, by sticking to the core principles that I have described so far—risk-based modeling, the January effect, and the 200-day moving average, you can run a great portfolio with tactical asset allocation in a proven system that can be repeated again and again and again.

ANNUITIES: SHINING SAVIOR OR DASTARDLY VILLAIN?

There is, perhaps, no topic more divisive around the investment community than annuities. Some people hate 'em; some people love 'em.

Susie Orman can't stand these investments. Yet, articles and research show that lifetime income is what people need. It can be so confusing.

We are going to explore two types of annuities: equity-indexed and fixed annuities. Why do some people like them? When are they appropriate? What are the pros and cons of this kind of annuity versus the other kind of annuity?

WHAT THEY DO

Overall, annuities are meant to be the exact opposite of life insurance. Life insurance pays a lump sum to beneficiaries for a stream of premiums, whereas annuities can pay a stream of income for a lump sum of premium.

HOW THEY WORK

There are two phases to annuities: accumulation and distribution. In accumulation, you put in money and let it grow. In distribution, you start to take out money.

Why do people like annuities? I can boil it down to two basic reasons:

THE PRIMARY ADVANTAGE

They can provide tax deferral outside retirement accounts. This means that you don't have to pay income and capital gains on an annual basis. This can lead to lower taxable income during your working years when you are accumulating dough. Delaying paying Uncle Sam is a good thing, right?

THE MAIN BENEFIT

Through annuitization, or with living-benefit and/or death-benefit riders on equity-indexed or fixed annuities, you can have insurance against downturns in the financial markets, ensuring a given asset value or cash flow stream of income. This kind of insurance company guarantee is something that a financial advisor like me could never offer an investor in a basic brokerage account where we invest in stocks, bonds, and other securities that can fluctuate up and down in price.

We'll discuss more about the bells and whistles of these annuity riders later in this chapter.

Now that you know the basics of why many folks like annuities, let's talk about why some people don't like them. While there are many cons to annuities, I will focus on the top two.

WHY ANNUITIES SUCK

First, most annuities have surrender charges. This means that if you want all of your money back after a year or two in the investment, you would get hit with a penalty for pulling out the money early. Note that some annuities have longer periods subject to surrender charges than others. Some have no surrender penalty, while many levy penalties for withdrawals taken within four, seven, or even ten years.

IT'S NOT A CHARITY

Second, the insurance company is in the business for a reason, which is to make money. Annuities are often more expensive than investing money in a brokerage account because, on top of a charge for living and death benefits, the insurance company charges for maintaining the annuity.

As an investor, you have to ask yourself whether you trust the markets to provide consistent rates of return, whether you can weather the ups and downs, and whether you have a sizeable cash cushion outside the annuity.

If you are not sure about the financial markets and you have a sizeable cash cushion or other investments, an annuity could be helpful.

However, just realize that your money could be tied up for some time and your maximum rate of return could be lower than if it were invested in brokerage accounts.

REMEMBER THIS

When using an annuity, use only a percentage of your liquid net worth. Consider using up to 40 percent, maximum, but less is generally better, the less you have in assets. I suggest to many clients that they allow plenty of leeway for the "stuff-happens" factors in life that could drain liquid assets. The less you have in liquid assets, the less money you should consider having in annuities.

Next, let's discuss the pros and cons of fixed and equity-indexed annuities.

FIXED ANNUITIES

Fixed annuities are fairly plain vanilla. Investors can earn a fixed rate that the annuity company will credit them, sometimes 2, 3, or 4 percent. This is very similar to CDs for investors, but without FDIC insurance. They earn a stated rate and won't go below a minimum guaranteed rate, usually 2 percent. Today, this is a lot better than can be earned in checking accounts or CDs.

HOW THEY MAKE MONEY

Just like a bank, the insurance company makes money here by earning a spread on its investments versus what it pays investors. The higher interest rates are like 10-year treasuries in that the more fixed annuities will tend to credit. Today, we are in a very low interest rate environment and thus I am not currently recommending fixed annuities to most clients because there isn't much reward with such a commitment.

WATCH OUT

In our current environment, be careful of teaser rates of 4 or 5 percent, or a special "bonus" rate, because they often revert back after one year to the minimum guaranteed rate.

Be sure to understand the length of the fixed annuities commitment, how much money you could walk away with at a minimum, and the minimum guaranteed rate. Watch out for annuities that force you into annuitization.

EQUITY INDEXED ANNUITIES

Meanwhile, equity indexed annuities (EIAs) have several characteristics. They have a floor, which is, typically, 0 percent; and a cap, which can range from 3 to 10 percent, depending upon the contract. These are declared annually and can change from year to year. I have found that, similar to fixed annuities, the higher 10-year treasury bonds are, the higher the cap rate is.

WHAT'S THE DIFFERENCE?

All in all, EIAs are very similar to fixed annuities in that they have a limited downside. Yet, at the same time, there is higher potential upside through partial stock market participation. What's even more interesting is that some equity-indexed annuities that don't have a cap have recently emerged.

Cap rates aside, equity-indexed annuities can participate in growth in different ways. You get to pick the index that you want the annuity to be marked to, whether the S&P 500 or the Dow Jones Industrial Average, or the Russell 2000.

KEEP IT SIMPLE

The annuity company will set a participation rate, which tells you how much of the gain you can participate in, up to the cap. I prefer contracts with a 100 percent participation rate to keep things relatively simple and easy to understand.

You get to decide how often you want to realize part of this growth: monthly, quarterly, or annually. I tend to prefer an annual point-to-point strategy for many reasons that we don't have time to cover in this text. Feel free to e-mail me for a breakdown of these reasons.

HOW THEY MAKE MONEY

Insurance companies make money on EIAs just like fixed annuities on a spread. The insurance companies make money by earning a spread on their investments versus what they pay investors. They hedge against some of the stock market risk and the higher crediting by buying futures and forwards on the indices that investors have selected.

HOW INSURANCE COMPANIES PROTECT THEMSELVES

They can limit their risk by changing the cap rate, participation rate, the indices that investors can select, and some other moving parts. Make sure to understand what can and cannot be changed for any investment you may consider in EIAs.

So, there you have it: a quick crash course on annuities. Now you know why many people like annuities and why many people don't like annuities. We've covered the pros and the cons as well as analyzing two major types of annuities.

HOW TO GENERATE INCOME FROM ANNUITIES

We just spent a good deal of time exploring two types of annuities: equity-indexed and fixed annuities.

THE OPPOSITE

Overall, annuities are meant to be the exact opposite of life insurance. Life insurance pays a lump sum to beneficiaries for a stream of premiums. Annuities can pay a stream of income for a lump-sum premium.

Now our attention is going to be focused on that stream of income. What are several ways to turn on that stream of income? What are the costs in doing so?

It boils down to this: with either equity-indexed or fixed annuities, you can have insurance against downturns in the financial markets and be sure you have a given asset value or cash flow stream of income.

But there's a cost. We'll talk more about that in a bit.

ALL ABOUT THE INCOME

You have two ways today of turning on guaranteed income from annuities: annuitizing the contracts, or using a living benefit rider.

Apart from those two ways, keep in mind that you should be able to withdraw money from a contract at any time, up to the penalty-free amount, although there may be penalties if you take out more than 10 percent during the surrender period.

There's no guarantee on the income stream. You take out what you take out, and if there's nothing left, you are screwed. On the other hand, if you are earning enough every year, I guess it doesn't matter.

I digress.

So, the primary two ways of getting income are . . .

THE OLD-FASHIONED METHOD

Annuitization is the good ol' traditional method that has been used since these kinds of investments began hundreds of years ago.

If you annuitize an annuity contract, you are being given an income for a given time period; it could be for a lifetime or, perhaps, for only a certain period of time.

WATCH OUT

Keep in mind that when you annuitize, you are giving up control of the money. Once that income stream is turned on, there is no looking back, whereas, before annuitization, you are still in the accumulation period and you can add or take out money as you please.

Once you annuitize, you are giving the money over to the insurance company *permanently* in return for the promise of an income stream. You can't take out more and you can't take out less. It becomes just like a pension or Social Security.

However, you do have certainty, and that's pretty awesome.

There are several different options that you have with annuitization.

1. You can choose to have an income stream for your lifetime. If you select that option, you will get the highest possible payout. However, the income goes away when you die.

2. Alternatively, you could choose the option of having it go partially or fully to a spouse. You get a slightly lower income than you do with the lifetime option if 50 percent goes to your spouse at your death, and a big pay cut if 100 percent goes to your spouse.

3. Also, consider that the later you start the income stream, the more income you will get. Most actuarial tables seem to plan to age 80.

So, if you have great health, you may want to wait until age 70 because you will lock in a way higher income stream than if you started at age 60.

Conversely, if you are in pretty cruddy health, you may want to start generating the income sooner rather than later.

I recently looked at annuitization for an ER physician who works with a big HMO on the West Coast. We looked at his getting income at age 65, and here's what we found:

Lifetime	50% to survivor	100% to survivor
$7,600/mo	$7,436/mo	$6,499/mo

See how there's a little bit of difference between lifetime annuitization and giving 50 percent to your survivor? It's only about $200/month, whereas giving 100 percent to your survivor means a pay cut of almost $1,100/month!

That being said, consider your specific situation. Is your spouse older or younger, in better or poorer health? Are you more likely or less likely to "beat" your spouse?

If your spouse is younger and in better health, whereas giving 100 percent to your survivor would make a lot of sense.

Okay, so that's enough about annuitization. I didn't have the space to cover the annuitization option of "period certain," but I think you get the idea.

Next, we'll discuss living benefit riders.

BUT I DON'T WANNA

The living benefit riders are a recent option for this historical investment. If you don't want to give up control of your money to the insurance company, they are the answer. The cool thing here is that living benefit riders allow you to maintain control of the money and still get a guaranteed income stream. They can be very confusing. So, tread lightly. Be aware of the provisions.

THE TWO CONFUSING TYPES OF MONEY

The riders can get a bit nuts when you start talking about two types of money.

The "contract value," or "surrender value," is the stuff that you can actually walk away with *anytime* versus the "living benefit" money, which you cannot walk away with and which your income is based on.

Warning: People start getting confused and maybe even suckered into buying these products when they hear about a "5 percent guarantee compounded for 10 years." Sounds great, right? But more often than not, this is a feature of the "living benefit" money, not the "contract value" money, which you can walk away with.

The insurance company doesn't give you the living benefit for free. It will usually charge around 1 percent, sometimes more and sometimes less, based on the value of the living benefit money, not the contract value.

Because most contracts have a built-in living benefit guarantee increase, your cost goes up every year before you start taking income.

So how do you get income from these living benefit riders?

HOW IT WORKS

The insurance company determines your guaranteed income by using a percentage based on your age, which is published in the annuity contract, multiplied by the "living benefit" money.

What is pretty cool is that you can withdraw amounts up to that guaranteed income percentage every year for the rest of your life even if the contract value drops to zero.

READ THE FINE PRINT

Things start getting sketchy when you withdraw more than the guaranteed income percentage allowed. Often, your guaranteed income will drop or can even go away if you do.

When you start taking the income, every year, you will still receive a statement showing your contract value/surrender value. You can walk away with this surrender value at any time, but if you do, you will no longer have the guaranteed income.

Nonetheless, outside that provision, there's some good stuff here.

Just as with annuitization, the older you are, the more income you get. The longer you hold a contract, the more your living benefit money can increase.

So, there you have it: a quick crash course on how to turn on an income stream from equity-indexed and fixed annuities. Now you know how you can do this, as well as the pros and the cons.

In this chapter, we have covered a lot, from asset allocation to annual highs and lows, the January effect, and much more.

But don't just take my word for it. Do some research on your own to validate or disagree with my theories.

In addition, check out resources at the end of this chapter.

CHAPTER SUMMARY

Asset allocation is the way in which you select your investments. It is meant to help match different kinds of investments to diversify them.

There are two basic types of allocation: strategic and tactical asset allocation. Strategic asset allocation doesn't change very much; it is fairly static. For example, an investor with a moderate risk tolerance may have a mix of 60 percent stocks to 40 percent bonds.

Meanwhile, tactical asset allocation can change very frequently. Managers try to be proactive in managing one risk or another. For example, they may be concerned about interest rates going up, so they may be shifting from long-term bonds to short-term bonds or to stocks.

Strategic asset allocation—buy, hold, and rebalance—means investors have to cling on, bare knuckles, white in the face, and swallow the losses that inevitably will happen from time to time.

History has taught me several basic rules of the road that you want to learn. First, it is not an aberration to have a year in which the market did not turn down. I believe this means we always need to have some money invested in stocks because there may never be a dip after the beginning of the year.

Second, if we are holding a fairly conservative allocation with only 15 to 25 percent invested in stocks, we should think about adding more to domestic stocks when the market drops 3 percent or more.

Third, we should expect about one out of every three years to end in a negative year and, about 40 percent of the time, we should expect a drop of 10 percent or greater from the price at the start of the year

In a positive 4 percent January, you must get invested. And not just partially invested. You must be fully invested according to your risk tolerance. You cannot wait. Otherwise, you could miss out on an average additional gain of 18 percent.

I would suggest that, even with a slightly positive January, it is still worth putting most, if not all, of your money to work in a traditional asset allocation model. If you do wait for a slight dip, that's okay. But don't wait too long and don't wait for a large dip because, for a huge percentage of the time, it will never happen.

All in all, the big ugly is significantly likely (but not guaranteed) to occur after a negative January. This makes it certainly worth your while to strongly consider waiting for a dip.

In my opinion, there are two technical indicators worth considering. First, the 200-day moving average of the S&P 500; and long-term price points, the five-year high and low for the S&P 500.

If the price of the S&P 500 is below the 200-day moving average, the trend is *negative*. You want to have a lower stock exposure.

If the price of the S&P 500 is above the 200-day moving average, the trend is *positive*. You want to have more stock exposure.

Annuities do have some benefits. First, they can provide tax deferral outside retirement accounts. Second, through annuitization, or with living benefit and/or death benefit riders on equity-indexed or fixed annuities, you can have insurance against downturns in the financial markets and be sure that you can have a given asset value or cash flow stream of income.

Watch out for surrender charges, fees, and other "gotchas" in annuities. The less you have in liquid assets, the less money you should consider having in annuities.

Annuities are meant to be the opposite of life insurance. They are meant to create an income stream. There are several ways to make that happen. First, you could consider annuitization. Alternatively, you can withdraw money from an annuity as you see fit. Lastly, the most recent addition to an annuity is a living benefit rider.

Each of these options has its pros and cons. It comes down to whether you want a guarantee, or you trust the markets or you want to have a bit of it all.

RESOURCES

If you would like to take part in a free webinar hosted by my partner Roger Anderson and me, make sure to check out my website at www.daviddenniston.com/investing-webinar.

Then, test your risk tolerance at www.daviddenniston.com/risk and get feedback on your portfolio.

Lastly, check out the books and websites that I referenced earlier in the text.

Stock Trader's Almanac by Hirsch, 2014 edition

The Ivy Portfolio: How to Invest like the Top Endowments and Avoid Bear Markets by Mebane Faber and Eric Richardson

Washington: A Life by Ron Chernow

Alexander Hamilton by Ron Chernow

Morningstar.com

VectorVest.com

CHAPTER 5

SEVEN CRITICAL MISTAKES DOCTORS MAKE WITH THEIR MONEY

Perhaps you are a young physician who has just come out of medical school. No more tests or studying. You've landed on your feet.

Maybe you are now in your residency or your fellowship and making a little bit of dough. You're starting to think about the future.

Perhaps you are a practicing physician who has made a few stumbles along the way and wants to make sure that you can avoid future pitfalls.

This special chapter is designed to help you learn from others' mistakes.

Cato the Elder (234 BC–149 BC) once said: "<u>Wise men profit more from fools than fools from wise men; for the wise men shun the</u>

mistakes of fools, but fools do not imitate the successes of the wise" (Plutarch, *Lives* at quotationspage.com).

Explore with me how you can minimize these mistakes and gain the knowledge you need for your specific situation.

This chapter was inspired by a post on the *White Coat Investor* blog. While I don't agree with everything there, that blog is a very worthwhile tool and offers some great education.

Dr. James Dahle, MD, who manages that blog, wrote the book titled *The White Coat Investor*, which is worth checking out.

In this chapter, we are going to address the following topics:

- Not Saving Enough For Retirement
- Not Having a Budget
- Lack of Patience and Discipline with Money
- Divorce
- Lack of (Good) DI Insurance
- Family and Friend Loans
- Starting Social Security Too Early and Not Maxxing Out Spousal Benefits

MISTAKE #1: NOT SAVING ENOUGH FOR RETIREMENT

We have talked a lot about debt already. Debt is incredibly important and should not be neglected.

However, I've seen too many people swing in the wrong direction and get so focused on debt that they have little to no savings for a "cash cushion," or retirement.

I thought James Dahle, MD, wrote succinct words of wisdom at WhiteCoatInvestor.com:

> Most people also have 40 years to save for retirement. Doctors only get 30 years, so they really need to be saving 15 percent if they plan to retire at 65.
>
> If you want to retire early, better bump that up to 20-25 percent. Remember, that isn't counting saving for your next car, that boat, a house down payment, or your kid's college fund. That's just retirement.
>
> A 5 percent savings rate just isn't going to cut it. So, on a $200K salary, that's $40K a year. Just putting $17K into your 401(k) each year isn't going to be enough.
>
> In short, you spend too much. Quit it. Like quitting smoking, it's simple, but not easy.

I want to add a couple of points to this commentary. If you are used to having an income of $200,000 and live on $100,000, your needs for retirement will add up quickly.

Consider this: *without inflation or taxes* or a rate of return on the money, 10 years of retirement and income needs costing $100,000 per year require a principal of $1 million. Twenty years of retirement needs costing $100,000 per year require a principal of $2 million.

If, instead, you can live on less—let's say $60,000 (again no inflation, taxes, or ROR), 10 years of retirement require a principal of $600,000 and 20 years of retirement require a principal of $1.2 million. Tack on an additional 10 years to retire even earlier or needing 30 years of retirement income and your principal needs to be $1.8 million.

See the difference? A retirement income of $60,000 requires way less savings; or, alternatively, save the same amount as someone needing $100,000 per year and retire way sooner.

Gather together information on your income needs and tax projections. Consider the rate of return on your investments and the inflation rate. Get a financial plan!

MISTAKE #2: NOT HAVING A BUDGET

I am shocked at the number of people I meet who live from month to month and don't keep track of their money. They know it comes in and goes out, ebbs and flows like the tide. They have some obligations they must meet and others they can cut.

You can be eons ahead of your peers just by simply understanding that flow. Know how much and when. I'm not talking about being a fanatic with a can't-cross-the-line kind of budget. It's all about knowing the flow so that if you have to, you know where you can cut.

My partner, Roger Anderson, had a client who was an MDA and who made $400,000 a year. He went to meet with him to discuss disability insurance (DI) and meet a gap in the group coverage. After a thorough review, we determined the DI coverage the client needed. After this recommendation, Roger said the client could not afford to pass up this coverage.

The client's response was shocking. The "gourmet club" was costing him and his wife $1,000 per month. It provided one gourmet meal for four couples. He said, "The gourmet club is killing me and my budget." He had to have the gourmet club and could not possibly give it up.

Don't be like this anesthesiologist. Understand what you can and can't cut from your budget. Understand the flows and make educated decisions. Take the next step to discover how much you can save without substantially changing your lifestyle. It is straightforward and easy to do on a monthly or bimonthly basis.

Sign up for eMoney Advisor or other software such as Mint or Quicken. Go to the section in the software that puts your monthly spending all together. For example, in eMoney Advisor, go to the Trends tab.

MISTAKE #3: LACK OF PATIENCE AND DISCIPLINE WITH MONEY

In my experience, physicians are some of the sharpest, most productive, tenderly compassionate, and wonderfully organized people. Yet, I find that many have the common characteristic of lack of patience and discipline with their money.

Unfortunately, investing, debt management, and insurance all involve a very long-term perspective. There's no prescription you can take to "cure" your portfolio after it has dropped 30 percent except to review and adjust and ride the roller coaster. Unfortunately, many people get off at just the wrong moment. Yet, somehow, some way, the market always rises to new heights within a few years.

I truly believe in asset allocation. You want to have a diversification of investments so that when one investment is doing poorly, another is doing okay.

Yet, some physicians start looking elsewhere because they are tired and frustrated by the stock market.

Some physicians have passive investments in all sorts of stuff: venture capital, wineries, equipment leasing companies, oil drilling companies, tax shelters, and burger franchises.

One of my physician clients invested in a winery in the Cayman Islands. He lost every single cent! Don't make a mistake like that!

Here are several criteria that you should consider with any investment:

1. Is it liquid? Can you sell it at any time and get at least a significant amount of money back?

2. Has it been registered or approved by the Securities and Exchange Commission (SEC), the Financial Industry Regulatory Authority (FINRA), or a state insurance commissioner?

3. Is it based or registered—for example, real estate, American depositary receipts (ADRs)—in the USA? No offshore tax shelters!

4. Could you manage it yourself if you had a poor manager?

I have one piece of advice for you: Keep it simple!

Ride the ride and be diversified. The traditional investments of stocks, bonds, real estate, ETFs, mutual funds, annuities, and cash-value life insurance all meet the criteria we have described.

They aren't always sexy or interesting or fun, but at least you can get a lump sum of cash at a whim.

Note that I do not endorse annuities or life insurance as good vehicles for many people, but at least they meet the four tests listed above.

Consider for a moment... what is the biggest mistake that you (or another physician/mentor/relative you know) have made with money?

MISTAKE #4: DIVORCE

"A happy, healthy marriage is not the result of luck, but rather that of both spouses being willing to make an investment of time and energy. Couples who work regularly to support each other and their marriage can build and nurture a lifelong relationship—those that get better with time" (Bruce Gilson, at marriageinvestment.com).

Many times in life we hit a rut. We get crabby and tired and feel unappreciated. We are busy and start feeling disconnected from our spouse. But we can do something about this.

Certainly, if your spouse is physically or verbally abusive, please make a change and get out of there. Otherwise, try and work it out as best you can.

Here are a few small tips to keep the fire going and to avoid divorce:

- Invest time and energy into your marriage. (Gals and Guys) Each of you plan a date monthly.

- Take a romantic trip, just the two of you, two times a year.

- Get counseling from time to time if various issues are gnawing at your marriage. It will be way cheaper than divorce.

Naturally, there are situations where many of us just can't work it out and man, is it heart-breaking.

There's nothing more destructive financially and emotionally that I have seen for clients than divorce. One household is split into two households. Kids torn down the middle. It can get ugly.

There's a great article on divorcesupport.about.com that addresses the cost of divorce.

In addition to what they say in that article, here are some key pointers to consider:

- **Can You Work Together and Keep the Attorneys Out Of It?** This is so hard to do—especially when you're talking about child support, custody, and how to divide your assets. There's a lot on the line. However, keeping more of what you have is a good thing! Work it out together, if at all possible—talk it out.

- **Be Open and Honest With One Another.** In my decade-plus career, I have seen some really cruddy situations. The hardest divorces happen when one spouse was hiding assets from the other spouse. One gentleman who was a client of our company spread his money across four or five different banks. Then, every few months, he would switch one or two of the accounts to another bank. He was so concerned about losing his hard-earned money.

  Yet at the end of the day, he ended up losing far more in the divorce settlement because of this deception. If we can all be open and honest with one another, lay all of our cards on the table, it is so much easier. It also saves months of back-and-forth communication between the attorneys and the court system.

- **Consider a Mediator.** Attorneys are sooooo expensive. The less you use them the better. Alternatively, think about using a mediator instead of an attorney. They are like a counselor, with specific training to handle disputes. Some specialize in divorces.

- **Get your financial advisor involved.** If you have a great advisor who knows your cash flow and assets in and out, have the advisor meet with each of you separately and then together. They can help with the asset division and really keep down the costs from the mediator and/or attorneys. A great advisor understands issues like 401(k) vs. Non-Qualified vs. IRA vs. Roth vs. Capital Gain Implications.

MISTAKE #5: LACK OF (GOOD) DI INSURANCE

First of all, this is not another plug for any insurance company. I am an independent financial advisor and wealth manager. I am not affiliated with any insurance company.

Regardless of whom you work with, make sure that you are working with someone who gives you a multitude of choices and educates you on the cheapest option as well as the most expensive option. Your advisor should empower you with the information necessary to make an educated decision on either life insurance or disability income insurance.

Frankly, in my opinion, insurance of all types is oversold. My basic philosophy is that you are most vulnerable when you most need insurance. I encourage you to save and save and save so that you no longer need an insurance company and can be "self-insured" down the road.

According to the Council of Disability Awareness and the Social Security Administration, illnesses such as cancer, heart disease, diabetes, back pain, injuries, and arthritis are common reasons for both long-term and short-term disability. Further, almost three in ten of today's 20-year-olds will become disabled before reaching age 67. That's 30 percent!

Additionally, the *American Journal of Medicine* (vol. 122, issue no. 8) reports that, every 90 seconds, someone files for bankruptcy in the wake of a serious illness.

This is a very real and present problem. According to the Standard Insurance Company, when disability does set in, the average duration is five to six years for someone who is less than 50 years of age.

How would your financial situation change if you weren't able to perform at your current capacity for five or six years? Voila! Disability income insurance was created to protect against this risk.

Are you a sole breadwinner or is your family a joint income family? What are your income needs? What would happen if you could no longer do your job? What do you have for group and individual disability insurance?

Check out or purchase the *Insurance Guide for Doctors Workbook* at Amazon.com for many ideas and a step-by-step guide to forming an action plan to minimize the cost of your DI or life insurance.

MISTAKE #6: FAMILY AND FRIENDS' ~~LOANS~~ GIFTS

We all love our friends and family. Well, most of them anyhow.

What happens when people win the lottery? All of their "extended family" and "friends," who never cared before, suddenly show up with hat in hand.

Then, guess what? These poor, foolish, generous souls, who never had money before, lose it in a heartbeat.

In your case, you've won a lottery too, although you earned your money through blood, sweat, tears, and hours and hours of studying and working for an average to below-average wage while accumulating debt.

Now, you are in practice and you are the "rich doc."

Hey, you have money right? Can't you help your dear Aunt Sally? She's going through a hard time.

But your sister just lost her job and your brother started a new business. So you lend $20,000 to dear Aunt Sally, $10,000 to your sister, and $50,000 to your brother. You can afford it, right?

No. You can't. You are not a bank. You are not going to do underwriting for, and credit checks on, friends and family. You do not have loan loss reserves. You're probably not even going to charge them interest.

Let's call a family "loan" what it is: a gift! I love helping people and I love giving gifts, but within reason. Would you give a $50,000 Christmas gift to your brother? Maybe $1,000 or $2,000 if you feel badly that he is going through hard times, or you believe in his business.

Give gifts and be a wonderful person, but don't give loans. Don't give personal loans! But be generous, and give gifts selectively to those you love and care about. Just don't expect the money back.

THE EXCEPTION

I was recently meeting with one of my retired physician clients in Washington state. We were overlooking the view from their beautiful home on a hill, taking in the crystal, calm surface of the Puget Sound.

I had known for years that they had given family loans to their kids, but they also gifted them tens of thousands of dollars along the way. Why did they decide to give them a loan? It goes against what I typically teach to clients.

As a matter of fact, those gifts were hundreds of thousands of dollars. They paid the kid's way through both undergrad and medical school. Both of their kids became doctors too!

As the kids finished residency and started practice, I found out that the family loans were to help them buy their first home. The kids had income, substantial income, and so they weren't worried about paying it back. Their kids are consistent overachievers and eager to please.

Additionally, my clients had more than enough resources that if the loans did default for whatever reason, they could write it off. Perhaps, in select situations, family loans are worth considering. But make sure you think long and hard about it before it happens.

MISTAKE #7: STARTING SOCIAL SECURITY OR PENSIONS TOO EARLY AND NOT MAXXING OUT SPOUSAL BENEFITS

We've covered a lot in this chapter. Let's wrap this up by focusing on retirement. Many physicians with whom I work tend to retire earlier than the average Joe because they are great savers and live well within their means.

However, I commonly see many physicians make the major mistake of starting a lifetime income stream by taking Social Security or pension benefits too early.

As many of us know, our life spans are getting longer and longer. We have new breakthroughs in medical technology every year. Is this trend likely to continue?

THINK ABOUT YOUR FAMILY

Consider your family's health history. How long has your father lived, your mother lived? How is your health? How is your spouse's health? Is it similar, better, or worse than your parents' health when they were the same age? Shouldn't you make a financial plan to cover the consequences of living longer?

Consider this scenario: your Social Security benefits are $1,250 per month at age 62, $1,800 at age 66, and $2,350 at age 70. Let's assume that there is no inflation or consumer price index (CPI) adjustment.

By age 71, you would have received the following benefits from each of these possibilities:

	SS started at 62	SS started at 66	SS started at 70
Total amount accrued	$135,000	$108,000	$28,200

By age 81, you would have received the following benefits from each of these possibilities:

	SS started at 62	SS started at 66	SS started at 70
Total amount accrued	$285,000	$324,000	$310,200

See the shift? By age 81, you would have been much better off if you had taken Social Security benefits at a later age. As you can imagine, the data looks better and better when benefits start to be paid at a later age.

THINK ABOUT HEALTH

I do want you to note that there is one special situation to be aware of. Consider very strongly the health of your spouse. Has your spouse had cancer, cardiac arrest, or other life-threatening health issues?

If your spouse has had health issues, consider starting to take Social Security benefits from the Social Security funds of the lower-earning spouse *sooner* rather than later.

Even if your spouse has never worked, he/she can claim up to half of your Social Security benefit.

Once you or your spouse passes away, the survivor will have the choice of taking the *higher* of the two Social Security incomes. One Social Security income will go away at the death of a spouse.

Thus, if you have a spouse in relatively poor health, don't wait! Start taking Social Security benefits from the Social Security funds of the lower-earning spouse as soon as possible.

However, if both of you are in good health, consider deferring taking benefits so that you can lock in a higher benefit for the rest of your life.

Go to ssa.gov, sign up, and download your most recent benefit statement. Do a break-even analysis to see if you would benefit from taking Social Security benefits at a younger age rather than an older age.

 BIG IDEA: Have you been part of a two-income household? Look into file-and-suspend!

Also, one other awesome strategy for married doctors that financial advisors don't bring up very often is file and suspend.

There's a few great article out there on this strategy. I particularly liked one from AARP that you can check out.

Overall, file and suspend is a really awesome strategy for married couples when one or both have been working. It's a way to start drawing on your retirement and earn some extra cash flow without touching one spouse's social security.

Crazy enough, both spouses end up drawing social security at the same time, but one of them still has a benefit that gets higher and higher until they turn off the "temporary income."

Here's how it works: At least one member of the couple must have reached full retirement age; this could be 65 up to 67 depending upon when you were born.

The rules are very complicated, but here's what the Social Security Administration website points out:

- If you and your current spouse are full retirement age, one of you can apply for retirement benefits now and have the payments suspended, while the other applies only for spouse's benefits. This strategy allows both of you to delay receiving retirement benefits on your own records so you can get delayed retirement credits. If you want to do this, only one of you can apply for retirement benefits and have the payments suspended.

- If you are already entitled to benefits, you may voluntarily suspend current or future retirement benefit payments up to age 70, beginning the month after the month when you made the request. They pay Social Security benefits the month after they are due. If you contact us in June and request that we suspend benefits, you will still receive your June benefit payment in July.

- You do not have to sign your request to suspend benefit payments. You may ask them orally or in writing. If your benefit payments are suspended, they will start automatically the month you reach age 70.

What does this all mean? Here's what this boils down to:

Let's say Jim just turned his full retirement age and he was the primary breadwinner for his family. Let's say that if he chose to take income now he could bring in $2,500/month.

However, if he delayed until age 70, those payments would be $3,200/month. That's $700 more a month.

Meanwhile, his wife, Kim, also just reached full retirement age. She worked on and off over the years. She worked early on, then stayed home with the kids for 10 years, then got a job again to help their cash flow. Her current benefit could be $1,200/month. If she delayed until 70, it could be $1,500/month.

Jim is in great health and enjoying life. Heck, his mom made is to 95 years old and his dad to 94. He has great genes.

As a brief aside, in a different scenario, if his income was way higher than Kim's than what we've shown (let's say $2,500/month for him compared to $700/month for her), what Jim could do is file for his full retirement benefits of $2,500 a month, and immediately suspend payment. He could then delay taking his own social security payments until age 70, when he would start to receive $3,200/month.

She could then file for spousal social security to take one-half of his benefit since that would be HIGHER than her benefit while he continues to wait on taking his benefits.

Then when Jim passes, Kim gets to continue his higher income and loses her relatively small benefit.

Anyhow, let's continue with this scenario.

In the meantime, while Jim is waiting to file for his primary benefit, Kim files for her own social security at $1,200/month and starts to receive that income.

Here's the crazy thing; when Kim filed for her benefits, it automatically activated the ability for Jim to apply for a spousal benefit.

Since Jim hasn't started taking his own social security yet, he could apply for the spousal benefit and take $600/month (one-half of Kim's) WITHOUT affecting his own social security.

It's free money with no strings attached!

Then, later on, Jim turns on his original social security benefit at $3,200 month and Kim can file for spousal benefits at $1,600/month. A total income of $4,800/month versus what they could have had on their own at $3,700/month at full retirement age.

In the meantime, they were still getting paid $1,800/month for three or four years while they waited to turn on that max benefit!!

If they didn't use this strategy, they would have left $65,000 to $80,000 on the table!

Let me sum this up in a few words: You are potentially leaving THOUSANDS of dollars on the table if you don't file and suspend and/or draw on spousal benefits.

You could be getting paid by the Social Security Administration without tapping into your benefit and, instead, using your spousal benefit for a few years while your *future* income from Social Security grows and grows.

Contact me at dave@daviddenniston.com if you would like access to the calculator that I use.

CHAPTER SUMMARY

There are six basic mistakes that I see physicians make with money that have not been addressed in earlier chapters.

Mistake #1: Not Saving Enough for Retirement

Dr. James Dahle, MD, said that "Most people have 40 years to save for retirement. Doctors only get 30 years, so they really need to be saving 15 percent if they plan to retire at 65."

If you want to retire early, you'd better bump that up to 20–25 percent. Remember that this isn't counting saving for your next car, that boat, a house down payment, or your kid's college fund. That's just retirement.

Mistake #2: Not Having a Budget

I am shocked by the number of people I meet who live from month to month and don't keep track of their money. They know it comes in and goes out, ebbs and flows like the tide. They have some obligations they have to meet and others they could cut.

You can be eons ahead of your peers simply by understanding that flow. Know how much and when. I'm not talking about being a fanatic with a can't-cross-the-line kind of budget. It's all about knowing the flow so that if you have to, you know where you can cut.

Mistake# 3: Lack of Patience and Discipline with Money

Stick to the basics. Make sure any investment in the markets you have is liquid and registered with the SEC or other similar body, meaning that you can sell it and there is some basic due diligence that has been done.

Mistake #4: Divorce

Many times in life we hit a rut. We get crabby and tired and feel unappreciated. We are busy and start feeling disconnected from our spouse. But we can do something about this.

Certainly, if your spouse is physically or verbally abusive, please make a change and get out of there.

Otherwise, try and work it out as best you can.

There's nothing more destructive financially and emotionally than divorce. One household is split into two households. Kids are torn down the middle. It can get ugly. There's a great article on divorcesupport.about.com that addresses the cost of divorce.

Mistake #5: Lack of (Good) DI Insurance

Frankly, insurance of all types is oversold, in my opinion. My basic philosophy is that when you are most vulnerable, you most need insurance. I encourage you to save and save and save so that you no longer need an insurance company and can be "self-insured" down the road.

How would your financial situation change if you weren't able to perform at your current capacity for five or six years? Voila! Disability income insurance was created to protect against this risk.

Are you a sole breadwinner or is your family a joint income family? What are your income needs? What would happen if you could no longer do your job? What do you have for group and individual disability insurance?

Mistake #6: Family and Friends' Loans

You are not a bank. You are not going to do underwriting for, and credit checks on, friends and family. You do not have loan loss reserves. You're probably not even going to charge them interest.

Let's call a family "loan" what it is: a gift!

I love helping people and I love giving gifts, but within reason. Would you give a $50,000 Christmas gift to your brother? Maybe $1,000 or $2,000 if you feel badly that he is going through hard times, or you believe in his business.

Give gifts and be a wonderful person, but don't give loans per-sonal loans! Be generous and give gifts selectively to those you love and care about. Just don't expect the money back.

Mistake #7: Starting Social Security or Pensions Too Early

I commonly see many physicians make the major mistake of starting a lifetime income stream by taking Social Security or pension benefits too early.

As many of us know, our life spans are getting longer and longer. We have new breakthroughs in medical technology every year. Is this trend likely to continue?

Consider your family's health history. How long has your father lived, your mother lived? How is your health? How is your spouse's health? Is it similar, better, or worse than your parents' health when they were the same age? Also, consider your spouse's health. One Social Security income goes away at the death of a spouse. It may be beneficial for a spouse in poor health to start taking benefits earlier rather than later.

Lastly, make sure to check out file and suspend and spousal benefits as a strategies, or you could leave a ton of money on the table.

RESOURCES

Go to http://www.PhysiciansRetire.com to download the complete guide of **Ten Critical Mistakes that Physicians Make with Their Money**.

We cover taxes, life insurance, and a few other topics in addition to the ones we have discussed here.

We also include a free, six-part video series (with a value of $19.79) as well as an offer to receive the DVD, **Financial Planning 101: The Financial Education You Never Got in Medical School**.

Check out or purchase the **Insurance Guide for Doctors Workbook** at Amazon.com for many ideas and a step-by-step guide to forming an action plan to *minimize* the cost of your disability insurance or life insurance.

For a financial blog by another physician, go to the WhiteCoatInvestor.com. Also, make sure to visit socialsecurity.gov to download your most recent Social Security statement.

Lastly, make sure to sign up for a budgeting program: Mint.com or eMoneyAdvisor.com. I can sign you up for eMoney Advisor. Make sure to contact me for access at dave@daviddenniston.com or (800) 548-1820.

SLASH DEBT & TAXES. CREATE A LIBERATED LIFESTYLE.

DOCTORFREEDOMPODCAST.COM

CHAPTER 6

EIGHT ACTIONS YOU MUST TAKE TO PROTECT YOUR SPOUSE AND KIDS

S omewhere over the rainbow . . . I can hear Judy Garland's soothing voice right now. Heaven, nirvana, the great after—that's where we would all like to be when we pass on.

Many of us enjoy the day-to-day moments, focusing on our families and growing wealth (then spending it) and we become so caught up in our busy lives that we don't take the time to ensure that our estates are set up properly.

It can be a big cluster of pitfalls if you don't take the proper steps.

We always say, "I'll handle that another time! I'll get to it another day." For example, it's estimated that more than 50 percent of people don't have a last testament and will!

In this chapter, we'll explore each of these topics:

- Have a Will and Know When to Get It Revised
- Learn about Probate
- Community Property vs. Common Property
- Federal Estate Taxes vs. State Estate Taxes
- TOD for Property
- TOD and POD Accounts
- Review over Beneficiaries and Stretch Provisions
- All about Trusts

Explore with me how you can minimize these mistakes with eight specific action steps to protect your spouse and kids.

ACTION #1: HAVE A WILL AND KNOW WHEN TO GET IT REVISED

Why should you have a will?

All in all, your will lets you decide how you want to distribute your assets and your estate. Without it, the state, rather than you, gets to figure out who gets what!

What if you have been divorced or have estranged kids? Do you want the state to decide that money should go to those folks?

Control your own destiny. Be the captain of your ship. The laws that govern what happens if someone does not have a will are called "intestacy laws," and they can vary wildly from one state to another.

In general, a spouse and kids receive their inheritance even when no will exists. But what if, instead, you are single and don't have kids? Then, the state gets to figure out which blood relatives get what.

If you are married and have kids who are under 21 years old, who will take care of them (who will be their "guardian?") and who will make that decision?

Who will be in charge of your financial estate? Will the kids inherit money at age 18 or is a trust with specific rules being set up on their behalf?

WHEN SHOULD YOU REVISE YOUR WILL?

As a general guideline, I suggest having it reviewed every 10 years.

This way you are keeping up with current laws and regulations.

However, if you have been through a major life event such as a divorce, new marriage, new baby, new stepchildren, death of a child, or a new grandchild, you will probably need to revise your will.

Keep in mind that IRAs, 401(k)s, annuities, and life insurance policies all declare specific beneficiaries. Make sure to review those beneficiaries. Make your spouse (if applicable) the primary beneficiary and have the kids (or their trust) listed as the contingent beneficiary.

Do you have a will? If not, create one!

If you do have a will, when was the last time it was reviewed? More than 10 years ago?

Review your will! Make sure it is current.

ACTION #2: LEARN ABOUT PROBATE

I am shocked by the number of people I meet who do not understand probate and its consequences.

Let's take some time to review this hair-pulling and time-clogging topic.

In essence, probate is the process of transferring property to heirs. A lawyer has to file all kinds of documents and place notices in newspapers and spend time and money to "fulfill" legal requirements.

Lawyers often charge a flat fee or a percentage of the estate value, which can range from 1 to 10 percent, depending upon the work required.

Think about it for a minute. Ten percent. That could add up to a lot of money! On a $1 million estate, 10 percent in charges for probate adds up to $100,000.

Basically, it's a scheme concocted by our legal system. There, I said it. Yes, it's a jaded view.

But that doesn't mean that you can't avoid it. As a matter of fact, there are several incredibly cheap (and even free) ways to avoid probate.

You'll need to understand the specifics of your state since states have varying rules.

Here are some of the questions you'll need to ask yourself:

1. Is my state a community property state?
2. Could I be subject to estate taxes? Do I fully appreciate that state estate taxes can be different from federal estate taxes?
3. Does my state allow a TOD for property?

4. How are my bank accounts and brokerage accounts titled? Are they TOD or POD? Do they have named beneficiaries?

5. What do I have in life insurance and annuities? Who are the named beneficiaries?

6. What do I have in IRAs, 401(k)s, Roth IRAs, and other retirement accounts? Who are the named beneficiaries?

7. Do I have a living trust or other type of trust? What assets are held within the trust?

Read more online about probate at http://www.nolo.com/legal-encyclopedia/ways-avoid-probate. Review the questions above and understand more about each of these in the next few steps.

ACTION #3: COMMUNITY PROPERTY VERSUS COMMON LAW PROPERTY

States follow one or the other of two basic legal structures regarding property: they are either community property states or common law property states.

In community property states, both spouses, equally, have rights to all assets. Essentially, everything gets split in half at the death of a spouse, even if the property title is under the name of one spouse only.

In the event of the death of a spouse, the state sees everything as a joint asset.

In comparison, in common law property states, the assets acquired by one spouse belong solely to that spouse and briefly stay this way at the death of that spouse.

These differences may seem very small, but could have a very large impact. This leads us to estate taxes. You could potentially save hundreds of thousands of dollars in estate taxes by utilizing the right vehicle.

COMMON LAW PROPERTY

For example, the state of Minnesota is a common law property state. It currently has a $1.2 million estate tax exemption. This means that the state will require an estate to file an estate tax return if any assets in the name of the deceased are over $1.2 million. This includes life insurance proceeds, 401(k) accounts, investment accounts, bank accounts, land, and so on.

People with a $1 million life insurance policy and $1.5 million in their 401(k) account have a $2.5 million estate and will be taxed on the amount over $1.2 million. In this case, that amount is $1.3 million.

In the state of Minnesota, taxes start at 10 percent and go up. An estate worth $2,500,000 would get hit with an estate tax bill of at least $130,000.

COMMUNITY PROPERTY

This brings us back to common law property states versus community property states. As a reminder, community property states, such as Texas or Washington, divide up the spousal assets equally at the death of the other spouse. Both spouses face the same estate issues.

In the previous example, let's say that the deceased spouse has no assets in his/her name. In a community property state, the same $2.5 million estate would be divided in half. The estate would be worth $1.25 million for each spouse. Thus, an estate tax exemption of $1 million leaves a taxable estate income of $250,000, which would be taxed at a rate of 10 percent, bringing the total estate tax bill to $25,000.

See the difference? It's an estate tax bill of $150,000 versus $25,000, simply dictated by the state where the couple resides.

Minnesota, on the other hand, looks at the assets in each spouse's name and keeps them separate. One spouse could potentially have an estate tax issue while the other does not.

Again, make sure you understand the estate limits for your state!

On top of that, there are also federal estate taxes. The exemption in 2013 was $5.25 million. As long as your estate is below that, you don't need to worry about federal estate taxes.

However, anything above that has a very steep tax of 40 percent. Keep in mind that the estate includes a life insurance death benefit (unless owned by an irrevocable life insurance trust (ILIT)).

I know, it's weird! But that's why you need to consult with a financial advisor and/or an attorney if you think you could have this issue.

Are you in a common law property state or a community property state?

RESOURCE:
Check out
http://divorce.lovetoknow.com/List_Community_Property_States
for more details.

Make a balance sheet and list in the rows every single asset that you own. Organize the columns under "His," "Hers," "Joint," "Revocable trust," and "Irrevocable trust."

Make sure to include the life insurance death benefit as an asset since we are looking at your estate at your death.

Write the dollar value of the asset under the proper column. For example, a 401(k) can only be in one spouse's column; it cannot be a joint asset.

ACTION #4: FEDERAL ESTATE TAXES VS. STATE ESTATE TAXES

As mentioned in our previous step, there are three different kinds of taxes to be aware of when somebody passes away: income taxes, federal estate taxes, and state estate taxes.

We are all familiar with income taxes; we pay them every day and file them every year. You'll end up needing to file a final income tax return for the deceased, as well as, possibly, an estate tax return. The bad news is that you cannot avoid income taxes.

However, the good news is that if your estate is set up properly, you can minimize or possibly avoid both federal and state estate taxes.

First, let's understand federal estate taxes.

As of 2014, there is a federal exclusion for the first $5.34 million of an **estate**. This means no federal estate tax is owed for the first $5.34 million of an estate.

Note that this includes all assets: the death benefit of an insurance policy, bank account money, 401(k)s, IRAs, Roth IRAs, your personal residence, and other real estate.

If your estate funds are over that exclusion, you need to be concerned with federal estate taxes, which can be very hefty: up to 40 percent of an estate!

Next, let's discuss state estate taxes. As mentioned previously, this same exemption amount can vary from state to state. For example, Kansas has no estate taxes, whereas Massachusetts has a very small $1 million exemption, and Washington has a medium $2,012,000 exemption.

Check out this hyperlink for more info: http://wills.about.com/od/stateestatetaxes/a/stateestatetaxchart.htm

This all leads to the penultimate question: if you are subject to estate taxes (federal or state), how do you avoid them?

Here are five specific strategies to consider:

1. **Annual gifting.** You can gift up to $14,000 a year tax-free to anyone. Keep in mind that gifting more than $14,000 a year could lead to gift taxes.

   This means you can gift to kids and grandkids and spouses and whomever else you desire.

   Let's say that you have two kids and four grandkids, and the kids each have a spouse. You have a total of eight people to each of whom you can gift $14,000, which comes to a total of $112,000 every year.

2. **Move to a different state.** Is there a better state or one with a warmer climate or one that has more favorable estate taxes where you would enjoy living in retirement? Review the chart that we mentioned earlier.

3. **Spend your assets.** Is your estate over that limit? Enjoy life! Take a few more trips. Check off your bucket list. See

your grandkids more often. Remodel your house! It's easy to spend money, but just be careful that you have enough to take care of your day-to-day needs until you are 90 or 100 years old.

4. **Irrevocable life insurance trusts (ILITs).** You can separate money from your estate by gifting annually to an ILIT. The death benefit from the insurance policy owned by an ILIT becomes separate from your estate.

   This way you can effectively transfer $500,000 or $1 million or $2 million that will not incur estate taxes as long as you play within the rules of the ILIT administration.

5. **Consider other estate planning techniques.** Similar to ILITs are family limited partnerships, charitable remainder trusts, charitable lead trusts, foundations, and numerous other vehicles. Also, you could separate a portion of your estate so that it is no longer included in your estate for estate tax purposes.

Understand your specific situation and how you fall within the federal and state estate tax exemptions. Make sure to review the previous step to understand whether you are in a common law state or a community property state and how it may affect your situation.

If you are over the exemption limits for the federal or state levels, make sure to review the five strategies that I have listed above.

Call me with questions about these strategies or what may work best for you. Each of them can be extremely complicated and should be coordinated with your financial plan to ensure that you have sufficient lifetime income to meet your needs as well as minimize or eliminate your estate taxes.

ACTION #5: TOD FOR PROPERTY

As we discussed earlier, probate can be a pain! There are many ways we have already discussed to avoid it.

Do you currently own real estate? Do you have a primary residence? Do you own rental properties?

For real estate holdings, there are two basic ways to avoid probate for any piece of property:

1. Have it owned by a living revocable trust

2. Get a transfer-on-death (TOD) deed

Once again, your ability to do one or the other can be restricted by where you live. The cheaper way to go is to get a transfer-on-death (TOD) deed.

A living trust is great! But then again, it can be extremely expensive, $1,000, $2,000, or more, depending upon the lawyer and your situation.

After you get the living trust, you have to file the proper form—a quit claim deed (in most states). Don't let the cost necessarily turn you away.

We'll talk more about the advantages of a living trust later.

However, if your situation is fairly simple, no issues with kids or dependents to be concerned with, the transfer-on-death deed is a very effective and simple tool.

In order to put it into effect, you must decide upon beneficiaries, much as you do with an IRA or life insurance, and list their addresses, dates of birth, and Social Security numbers on the form.

Upon your death, the property *automatically* bypasses probate and transfers right to the beneficiaries.

There are currently 22 states that allow you to get a transfer-on-death deed. Check out the hyperlink below for more details:

http://www.nolo.com/legal-encyclopedia/free-books/avoid-probate-book/chapter5-1.html

Do you currently own real estate?

Do you have a simple situation?

Utilize a transfer-on-death deed to avoid probate.

ACTION #6: TOD AND POD ACCOUNTS

Besides applying TOD to real estate, you can apply the same principle of TOD to any nonqualified account at a bank or a brokerage company. Many banks call it paid-on-death (POD). I have found it to be a free service available at any bank. You keep the same account number and title and sign the POD form, which lists the primary and contingent beneficiaries.

You also automatically avoid probate by having an asset jointly held. My wife and I make sure that we are *jointly* on all our bank accounts. Kids can easily do this with parents, just as spouses do.

In cases where we cannot be jointly listed, we make sure the account is a POD. In the investment world, we call it transfer-on-death (TOD). Again, this should be a *free* service at any investment company.

Keep in mind that it only applies to *nonqualified* accounts.

This means that it does not apply to 401(k)s, 403(b)s, IRAs, Roth IRAs, annuities, or life insurance policies, since they already automatically declare beneficiaries.

As mentioned earlier, if your situation is fairly simple—no issues with kids or dependents to be concerned with—the transfer-on-death designation is a very effective and simple tool.

In order to put it into effect, you decide upon beneficiaries, much as you do with an IRA or life insurance, and then you list their addresses, dates of birth, and Social Security numbers on the form.

Upon your death, the account *automatically* bypasses probate and transfers right to the beneficiaries.

Review your bank accounts and investment accounts. Make sure that they are jointly held and/or are POD or TOD, respectively.

ACTION #7: REVIEW BENEFICIARIES AND STRETCH PROVISIONS

The next step is to go over each and every one of your accounts, make sure they have named beneficiaries, and ensure that all is in order. Keep in mind that IRAs, 401(k)s, annuities, and life insurance policies all declare specific beneficiaries.

What if you don't list any beneficiaries or indicate "per my will" as the beneficiary? The assets *do not* bypass probate.

Therefore, make sure to fill in the details. Make your spouse (if applicable) the primary beneficiary and list the kids (or their trust) as the contingent beneficiary.

If your spouse is listed as the primary beneficiary, the assets can automatically transfer to an IRA in that spouse's name, or your spouse can keep the existing IRA as a "descendant spousal" IRA.

You may want to use a descendant spousal IRA in order to stretch the required minimum distribution over a younger spouse's longer life expectancy. If your spouse is older than you are, you will likely be better off consolidating the IRAs.

Let's say that instead of a spousal IRA, we are talking about an inherited IRA in which kids or grandkids inherit money right from the parents/grandparents. Here is a very important point that I want to make: *name your contingent beneficiaries.*

Ninety-five percent of clients whom I have dealt with come in with a primary beneficiary listed. I consider that a nonissue.

But only about 50 percent of those clients come in with a contingent beneficiary listed. It's easy to overlook. Or even worse, a spouse has passed away and the beneficiaries were never changed.

Keep in mind that if you are concerned about how kids or grandkids may treat the money, you can name a trust for an irresponsible child in order to control how much and for what purpose money can be withdrawn.

I strongly suggest consulting an estate planning lawyer to ensure that the beneficiaries are properly named.

There are some fantastic stretch provisions for the kids and grandkids (or their trusts) named as beneficiaries.

Once they inherit an IRA account, they have to start taking a required minimum distribution (RMD). The amount will be based off their life expectancy rather than the grantor's life expectancy.

For example, let's say that Grandpa Joe has a $300,000 IRA on December 31, 2014. He will have turned 80 years old when he passes away on January 1, 2015. Grandma Josephine passed away years earlier.

His only child, Joseph Junior, turns 45 years of age, and his only grandchild, Evangeline, turns 15 years of age this year.

Both of them were listed as primary beneficiaries and split the assets 50/50.

If Grandpa Joe has to take out a RMD in 2015, it will have to be for *a total of $16,042* in 2015.

Meanwhile, Joseph Junior, with his inherited RMD, only needs to take out $4,385 and Evangeline, $2,210, for *a total of $6,595*.

See how they can stretch the tax obligation out over a longer period of time and allow the assets to continue to grow?

Review the beneficiaries for all of your retirement and tax-deferred accounts. Make sure that primary and contingent beneficiaries are named.

ACTION #8: ALL ABOUT TRUSTS

We've now gone through many ways to avoid probate and protect your family from probate. What if you need to protect your family members from themselves? Sometimes we can be our own worst enemy.

For example, I love my cousin. He is the sweetest person in the world. He has a heart of gold. He would give away the last strip of clothing off his back to somebody in need. He gives and he gives and he gives but, unfortunately, to his own detriment at times.

He has dealt with a lot in his life but simply hasn't developed various life skills. He doesn't have the drive to succeed that many of us do. He can't hold a full-time job and had to declare bankruptcy once, almost twice if he hadn't been bailed out by his parents.

I find more and more clients are helping their kids in retirement. Perhaps it's because of a bad economy. Perhaps it's because of a lifestyle choice. I'm not quite sure.

Many people are very concerned with how their kids would spend money if they inherited it. They want to protect their money from divorces and greedy spouses and, sometimes, from the kids themselves.

This is why various forms of trusts exist. You can dictate how much and where funds can go.

For example, your trust can specify, at your death, the formation of an irrevocable trust for the care of a named beneficiary. That beneficiary can only spend 3 or 4 percent (or whatever you choose) of the assets per year—so that you can ensure that the beneficiary will have an income for the rest of his/her life.

This can protect the kids from the divorces and even from themselves.

Some people use trusts to avoid public disclosure in the court system. With the living trust, you have the advantage of keeping your affairs private.

With a traditional will, everyone can see what was transferred to your beneficiaries when court documents are filed.

Also consider what we discussed earlier about real estate TODs. Only 22 states grant the ability to use real estate TODs. The other 28 states force the use of living trusts as a way to bypass probate for real estate holdings.

Are you concerned about some of the issues we have mentioned? Talk to an estate lawyer about a living revocable trust or other vehicle.

CHAPTER SUMMARY

Action #1: Have a Will and Know When to Get It Revised

All in all, your will lets you decide how you want to distribute your assets and your estate. Without it, the state gets to figure out who gets what rather than you!

Control your own destiny and be the captain of your ship. The laws that govern what happens if someone does not have a will are called "intestacy laws," and they can vary widely from one state to another. In general, however, spouses and kids receive their inheritance even when there is no will.

Action #2: Learn about Probate

In essence, probate is the process of transferring property to the heir(s) of the deceased. A lawyer has to file all kinds of documents and place notices in newspapers and spend all this time and money to "fulfill" legal requirements. Lawyers often charge a flat fee or a percentage of the estate value, which can range from 1 to 10 percent, depending upon the work required.

Action #3: Community Property versus Common Law Property

There are two basic kinds of legal structure pertaining to property, one or the other of which is followed by state governments. There are community property states and common law property states. In community property states, both spouses equally have rights to all assets. Essentially, everything gets split in half at the death of a spouse even if the title is under the name of only one spouse. In the event of the death of that spouse, the state sees everything as a joint asset.

In comparison, in common law property states, the assets of one spouse belong solely to that spouse and briefly stay this way at death.

Action #4: Federal Estate Taxes versus State Estate Taxes

First, let's understand federal estate taxes. As of 2014, there is a federal exclusion for the first $5.34 million of an estate. If your estate funds are over that exclusion, you need to be concerned with federal estate taxes, which can be very hefty, up to 40 percent of an estate!

Next, let's discuss state estate taxes. As mentioned previously, this same exemption amount can vary from state to state. For example, Kansas has no estate taxes, whereas Massachusetts has a very small $1 million exemption, and Washington has a medium $2,012,000 exemption.

Action #5: TOD for Property

With property, the cheaper way to go is to get a transfer-on-death (TOD) deed. In order to put it into effect, you must decide upon beneficiaries much as you do with an IRA or life insurance and then you must list their addresses, dates of birth, and Social Security numbers on the form. Upon your death, the property automatically bypasses probate and transfers right to the beneficiaries.

Action #6: TOD and POD Accounts

Besides real estate, you can apply the same principle of transfer-on-death (TOD) to any nonqualified account at a bank or a brokerage company. Many banks call it paid-on-death (POD). In my experience, this is a *free* service available at any bank. In the investment world, we call it transfer-on-death (TOD). Again, this should be a free service at any investment company.

Action #7: Review Beneficiaries and Stretch Provisions

The next step is to go over each and every one of your accounts to be sure you have named beneficiaries and to ensure that all is in order. Keep in mind that IRAs, 401(k)s, annuities, and life insurance policies all declare specific beneficiaries. What if you don't have any listed beneficiaries, or indicate "as per my will" as the beneficiary? The assets *do not* bypass probate.

Action #8: All about Trusts

Many people are very concerned with how their kids would spend money if they inherited it. They want to protect their funds from divorces and greedy spouses and sometimes from the kids themselves. This is why various forms of trusts exist. You can dictate how much and where funds can go. For example, your trust can specify, at your death, the formation of an irrevocable trust for the care of a named beneficiary who can only spend 3 or 4 percent (or whatever you choose).

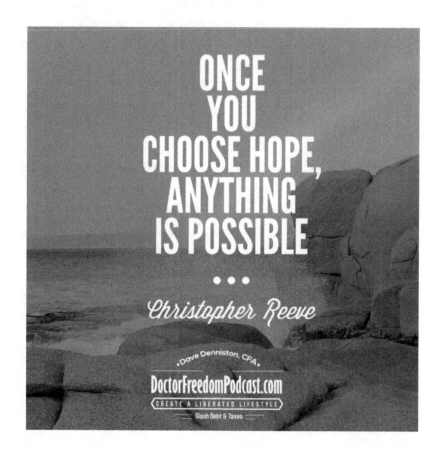

FINAL THOUGHTS

Congratulations! You've just accomplished something that very few people have ever done in their lives. You have taken the time to invest in your future by reading this book. You have explored time-tested strategies on debt, taxes, investments, and insurance.

You've learned about important subjects from forming a financial roadmap and plan to five ways to reduce your income to Roth IRA conversions to tactical asset allocation to social security.

Take the next step: implement the tools that you have learned. Ask for help. We cannot control many things in our lives: the weather, our favorite sports team winning the big game, being sick, a family member passing away, children who make poor decisions, and so much more.

However, your finances and how you treat them are in your power. Take control today. Live within your means. You can do it! I encourage you to revisit this book on an annual basis. I will make updates based on your feedback. So, please let me know your experience and where I can improve.

Finally, for the COMPLETE Freedom Formula for Physicians System, check out page 220.

Are you curious to hear about the feedback from other doctors about the Freedom Formula System? Check out the NEXT PAGE to hear directly from physicians who are just like you.

If you would like any additional support and to learn more about how I can serve you, please feel free to contact me anytime at dave@daviddenniston.com or call me at (800) 548-1890.

Let's take this journey together and get you on the path to financial freedom.

Warm Regards,

Dave Denniston

PRAISE FOR THE FREEDOM FORMULA FOR PHYSICIANS

"What I appreciate about Dave's advice is that it is reflective of my own values. He takes the time to listen and get to know me before he offers his own insight. This makes discussing financial matters comfortable and enjoyable."

—David Arens, MD, Podiatry

"As I neared the completion of my residency, I realized I was about to start in a whole new phase of life. I felt very comfortable with my medical training and felt prepared to take care of patients. Unfortunately, I felt grossly unprepared to manage my newly improved income or to dig out of debt. I also was faced with all kinds of decisions including malpractice insurance, life insurance, retirement accounts, taxes, loan consolidation/repayment, and so on. Thankfully, it was at this time that I met Dave. He has been an invaluable resource to help me navigate each of these issues and many more. He is trustworthy, knowledgeable, and patient, and I would recommend him to anyone in a similar situation."

—Kyle Klingler, MD, Ophthalmology

"Dave's advice is very valuable because he is so familiar with the unique financial challenges that come with being a physician. I feel that my husband and I are in good hands with Dave."

—Gretchen Vanden Berg, MD, Family Medicine

"Dave has a deep understand of how to be successful and get the most out of your investments. He is patient and kind. Everyone who has the opportunity to team up with him is lucky. You can be confident he will do his best for you."

—Kimberly Workman-Patterson, MD
and Jeffrey Patterson, Orthopedic Surgeon

"I especially appreciate Dave's advice that includes at times three options, which he explains thoroughly. He is aware of our personalities and goals and tailors his approach in a concerned and caring manner. We value and appreciate his friendship and stewardship of our assets...

His advice for [my wife] and I during our retirement has been valuable. We tend to be very conservative and his advice to spend some money and live a full life has been most helpful ...

I highly recommend Dave Denniston to anyone who can profit from advice not only financially, but in mapping out a pathway toward a secure retirement."

—George G. Hodge, MD
Retired Orthopedic Surgeon

"My husband and I contacted Dave soon after getting married to help us create a foundation around finances and to help guide us regarding resolving credit card debt, managing stock investments, managing school loans, creating a budget, and reviewing job contracts. He has been WONDERFUL! He is through, reliable, and very sensible.

He met us wherever we were at and step by step guided us through several decisions. We look forward to a long relationship with him."

—Neha Kramer, MD & Christopher Kramer, MD
Neurologists

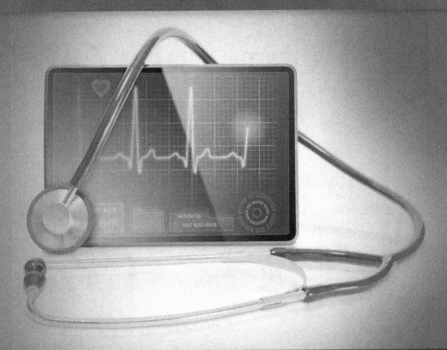

Printed in the USA
CPSIA information can be obtained
at www.ICGtesting.com
JSHW012050140824
68134JS00035B/3357